love you,
ster. i hope
is makes you
ugh as much as you
ake me laugh.

Merry Chr

-K

Scraps

Scraps:

ADVENTURES IN SCRAPBOOKING

Wendy Bagley

HYPERION

NEW YORK

Library of Congress Cataloging-in-Publication Data

Bagley, Wendy.
  Scraps : Adventures in scrapbooking / Wendy Bagley.
    p. cm.
  ISBN 1-4013-0216-5
  1. Photograph albums.   2. Scrapbooks.   I. Title.

TR465/N34 2005
745.593—dc22   2005050392

Hyperion books are available for special promotions and premiums. For details contact Michael Rentas, Assistant Director, Inventory Operations, Hyperion, 77 West 66th Street, 11th floor, New York, New York 10023, or call 212-456-0133.

FIRST EDITION

10   9   8   7   6   5   4   3   2   1

This *book is dedicated to*

THE WINEGARS,

& THE BAGLEYS,

& THE COFIELDS

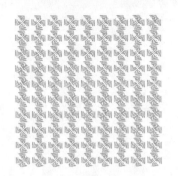

Contents

Contents

VIII

Contents

ix

Contents

x

Acknowledgments

Scrapbookers are life savers—they save life's memories from fading away. They create original legacies of love using little more than photographs, patterned papers, pens, punches, embossers, stampers, staplers, rulers, scissors, stickers, stencils, scanners, sequins, ribbons, protectors, printers, eyelets, templates, trimmers, cardstocks, wires, fibers, fonts, die-cuts, dots, chalks, charms, mats, metals, buttons, beads, brads, borders, glitters, grippers, glues, inka dinka doos, vellums, laminators, adhesives, albums, an assortment of other cropping tools, a vast selection of stamps, every embellishment imaginable, and a slew of gadgets including a rotating ball-bearing disc.

Currently, some would say tragically, I lack the unique knack necessary for successful scrapbooking. This is not a federal offense or anything, but it upsets me and it upsets my children.

(We are easily upset; for example, when *The Simpsons* is pre-empted, we throw a fit.) Nevertheless, my ineptitude was nowhere near enough of an obstacle to keep me from drawing on the rich experiences of talented scrapbookers to whom I am related or with whom I have related, and revealing what crops up in their scrapbooking lives—lives filled with boundless creativity and astonishing originality.

Some of these essays were written as tributes, some were written as spoofs, yet all were written on a laptop computer as a means of exploring the heart and spirit of scrapbooking and the positive effect it has on individuals, their families, their communities, and the world at large.

My primary goal here was to write a comprehensive book that celebrates the adventures of human beings on the cutting edge; a collection of essays that extols scrapbookers' accomplishments without making me sound foolish, insecure, or, worse, envious. [Editor: This is not that book.] Writing an exclusive, somewhat inclusive, relatively effusive book about scrapbooking required (1) relentless effort, (2) the continual use of a thesaurus, and (3) a dietary increase of seven of the eight essential amino acids. It practically goes without saying that I worked diligently—very diligently. Little by little, line by line, day in and day out, I would write about scrapbooking until I had what felt like a good paragraph. And so it went, week after week. It took a lot of time; it took a lot of words. In fact, this collection of scrapbook essays would have been available in bookstores months ago but for the fact no publisher would consider a manuscript with fewer than 40,000 words. Now, more than 38,000 words later, here is one of the best scrapbooking books ever written on what is presumably acid-free paper.

Now, on with the acknowledged purpose of an Acknowledgment page. I am most grateful to Philip Cofield for his faith in me over the years. It would be a blessing to even know him, and here he's my husband.

I also want to thank some of the funniest people I know and love: Alison McFarlane, Judith Payne, Dorothy Maryon, Mari-anne Mueller, and Carolyn Bringhurst for their encouragement and advice.

And to the many scrapbookers who shared your stories if not your names, thank you.

Jenny Bent, my agent, and Kelly Notaras, my editor, are just wonderful. I owe them an extraordinary debt of gratitude for their life-changing support and encouragement.

My heartfelt appreciation also goes to the talented Jane Wilcox, Judy Winegar, Heather Erickson, and Kim Winegar. True scrappers all, they gave me inspirational stories and an overde-veloped sense of being inferior. I am also deeply indebted to my sweet mother, Norma Jean, whose recommendation that this book be published posthumously I chose to ignore.

For her contributions both verbal and written, I am most grateful to Susan Winegar (aka "Editor" throughout), who made every attempt to tidy up this collection of essays long before a professional editor came along and made them readable. A bet-ter person you will not find; a kinder sister I could not have. (Why I could not have a kinder sister, God only knows.) Without her splendid wit and vast generosity, this tragicomedy—this slim volume bound to be a scrapbooking classic—would not have been written. She told me not to mention it; in fact, she requested I not mention her at all in connection with this book. However, without acknowledging her contributions there would be no one to blame but myself.

Scraps

CHAPTER 1

Holyscrapoly!

Scrapbooking is addictive. Just ask a scrapaholic, a stampaholic, a cropaholic, or my sister. More than scrapbook "oriented," these photo lovers are scrapbook *obsessed*—which, if you ask me, rhymes with *stressed*.

Yet ask a scrapbooker and she'll say *blessed*.

Scrapbookers are indeed lucky. Lucky to be addicted to something that makes them so happy. Off the top of my head I can think of only two other hobbies that make people as genuinely joyful as scrapbooking. One, as you've probably already guessed, is balloonology—that's where nimble-fingered people twist balloons into animal shapes. The other is showing kindness. Except for a handful of clowns and the Dalai Lama, very few individuals are addicted to either one of these activities.

Scrapbooking, however, is highly addictive. Just take a look at my aforementioned sister, who is bright, uptight, and can stay up all night when she's scrappin'. Eventually, however, her increased craving for more cropping made her kind of crazy. Exactly how crazy became clear recently when she signed us up for an all-night, nonstop crop party. She arrived with her film so tightly wound that, in a flash, she just snapped: Snap! Snap! Snap! Repeatedly, picture after picture. Then this multitasking, photo-basking scrapper began circling the room like a whirling dervish. She chalked and talked, punched and munched, inked and winked, and stamped until her fingers cramped. [Editor: Somebody else we know suffers from rhyme disease and the inability to let another person edit her writing.] Touché! Anyway, by the time she started tinting, she was squinting. Even though she looked tired she claimed to be wired and refused to call it quits. The next morning we found her fast asleep, facedown in a pile of brads, a fine film on her forehead, deeply indented with tiny "o" marks.

Oh, what does one do when someone one loves is addicted to scrapbooking? You cannot drive her to Scrapaholics Anonymous, since there is no such thing. Why? For the simple reason that anonymity is the farthest thing from a scrapbooker's mind. You can't take away her supplies unless you rent a U-Haul truck. You can't say W*hoa*! C*ut it out*! because she is a nut for cutting; cutting things out is the very sort of activity that contributes to her scrapbooking obsession in the first place. So the best you can hope to do by way of helping a scrapaholic is to encourage her to join a good support group. That is exactly where my sister ended up. Now she frequently goes away to retreats, weekend crops, stamp camps, and scrapbooking conventions where she reportedly gets all the help and page ideas she needs when it comes to facing and embracing her beloved addiction.

Does this sound a little too familiar? I knew it! You wouldn't be holding this book in your hands unless you were yourself somewhat addicted to scrapbooking. (Or could find nothing better to read in the bathroom.)

To determine beyond a doubt whether you are a scrapaholic, spend a few strange minutes answering the following CROP QUIZ:

Q: Do you tend to use excessive exclamation points even when writing something as basic as a personal check?

Q. Do you refer to scrapbooking time as "Happy Hour"?

Q. Do the people in your dreams have enormous heads and stick-figure bodies?

Q. Does your T-shirt, license plate, and/or tattoo boast the phrase "Scrapper Girl"?

Q. Do you need a little "night scrap" to get to sleep?

Q. Do you perform a brief victory dance each time you complete a scrapbook page?

Q. Do you take multiple photographs of parade floats, fireworks, and zoo animals?

Q. Do you enjoy systematically cataloging stacks of color-coordinated and patterned paper while alphabetically arranging thousands of decorative items according to theme, season, and texture?

Q. Did you remember to grab a camera the last time you rushed out the door, wounded and bleeding child in your arms, on your way to the hospital emergency room?

Q. Does your right hand always know what your left hand is doing?

Q. Have you canceled hair appointments, Botox treatments, or lunch engagements to help defray the cost of your scrapbook supplies?

Q. When asked, "What do you say?" do your children answer "*Cheese!*"? (Note: Correct response would be "Please" or "Thank you.")

Q. When your spouse suggests you find a way to cut corners, do you assume he is proposing a possible page-design technique? Alternatively, do you shake your decorative scissors menacingly in his direction?

Q. Is your fondest wish to get into Harvard Law School? (No, wait. Ha! That's a question for the readers of the other book I'm trying to write.)

Q. Are you depleting your children's college fund to pay for your scrapbook supplies?

Q. Have your last six family vacations included Hobby Industry Association conventions?

Q. Do you think "lunatic fringe" is a page border?

If you answered *yes* at least three times or clapped your hands in glee more than once, you're a certifiable scrapaholic. Now is the time to get support, join a group, or call my sister—unless you *are* my sister, in which case you should call me so I may apologize for revealing your addiction without your permission.

CHAPTER 2

A History of Scrapbooking

Anyone who thinks scrapbooking is just a fancy pastime or a passing fancy has never heard the laughter of a daughter as she opens her scrapbook's cover; never seen the joy of a boy as he turns his scrapbook's pages; never witnessed the wild-eyed glee of a scrapper gal as she forks over her family grocery money in exchange for photo albums and stacks of patterned paper.

Ladies and gentlemen, scrapbooking is here for good. Only those who fail to pay attention to the big social developments in the world would deny that this creative hobby has forever changed the everyday behavior of women, men, and children. Even family pets stand in red-eyed alert, sensing that at any moment—*whrrrrzzz! flash!*—they could briefly lose their eyesight and control of their bladder as the scrapbooker in the house takes advantage of yet another photo opportunity.

All of which makes it difficult to believe that scrapbooking mania didn't take hold the instant consumer-friendly cameras were offered to the public. By and by, however, human beings stopped being oblivious to joy, and the idea of snapping pictures clicked. It helped that as progress was being made in the camera department, both photographic equipment and photographic people were becoming much easier to manipulate. Around this same time professional photographers realized it was time to stop insisting that everybody *please, just settle down and be serious.*

People posing for photographs, however, appeared only too happy *not* to smile. Back then everybody wanted to be taken seriously, or at least they wanted a serious portrait taken. Except for babies, humans were disinclined to smile on purpose while sitting in front of a camera. Early on, from time to time, a person might nervously raise the corners of his or her mouth, but it rarely looked natural or made any sort of point. This is the reason we have so many of those old sepia photographs showing our ancestors looking dead serious. [Editor: What kind of researcher are you? People didn't smile back then because daguerreotypes took ten to twenty minutes to shoot, and people can't smile that long without moving.]

Thank you, Miss Know-it-All! "*Daguerreotypes!*"—how very *fascinating.* But beside the point, which is that those old photographs are beautifully haunting. One of my personal favorites is a portrait showing my grandmother and her siblings as children dressed in their churchgoing clothes and standing in the parlor of their childhood home. By the looks on their faces you would think the photographer, just moments before clicking his camera—

oh, *pardon me*, I mean his *daguerreotype*—had twisted his waxed mustache upward, then sneered, "Nobody move, nobody smile— your parents want me to shoot you!"

Over the years, both behind and in front of the camera, people became much better at relaxing as they grew more comfortable with the whole idea of candid photography. It was not long before a lot of candid people—from, I believe, Canada—began requesting and receiving cameras for their birthdays and calling themselves "shutterbugs." Naturally, all of this activity led to thousands of snapshots of everything from Grand Canyon vacations to grandchildren's graduations. Pretty soon all of these photos started stacking up around the house until people had no choice but to toss them into empty shoeboxes and sock drawers.

Then—according to a photo-fiend friend of a friend—one day a man named Albert (not the prince) was fixing a leaky pipe under the kitchen sink when his wife, as a joke, took a picture of his substantial backside, which was showing just a crack. Well, as you can imagine, that photograph made a lot of people laugh out loud. After all, this was the late '50s, and visual humor was nowhere near as sophisticated as it is today. R*ight*.

Albert, who did not mind being the butt of a joke, put the photo in a book for safekeeping and easy access. Eventually, the book containing Albert's photo came to be called *The Book of Al's Bum*, which soon was shortened. As in, "The bishop could use a good laugh, go fetch the Al's Bum book!"

Inspired by the photo-in-book idea, Albert's oldest son soon started a little business that sold the world its first photo Al-bum.

Within no time, much of the picture-taking population was

filling up photo albums left and right without a care in the world. Until somebody who happened to know a little bit about lignin and acid said, "For Pete's sake [Pete being her only child], for the sake of future generations, for the love of all we hold dear, let us preserve our memories on photo-friendly paper or surely our efforts will fade with the passing of time!" She was a bit of a nut, but a well-meaning nut. [Editor: Takes one to know one.]

So photo-safe supplies were invented, and everyone with a brain in her head and film in her camera ran out to stock up on acid- and lignin-free products. Then one thing led to a million decorative things (called embellishments), and the rest, as they say, is scrapbook history. Or hysteria. However you want to look at it. Anyway, you get the picture, and a big picture it is.

Never in the history of the world has there been a hobby as popular as scrapbooking! [Editor: Excuse me? This simply is not true. Knitting, woodworking, stamp-collecting, gardening, calligraphy, soap-carving, knot-tying, doll collecting, and origami, to name but a few, are more popular than scrapbooking.] Well, whoop-de-doo-dah! Just because a hobby is a little more popular does not make it any more noble or worthwhile than scrapbooking, which, nobody can deny, is the best-*loved* hobby of all. And it is growing by leaps and bound albums, thanks to scrapbookers who, themselves, couldn't be more popular.

Filled with one cheerful obsession after another, scrapbookers are glued to the notion that happiness and a well-documented life go hand in hand. They are out there taking pictures as if there's no tomorrow, so as to joyfully connect generations past and present. Their love of family and their spirit of creativity spread all the way from California to the New York Island—to somewhere out there close to perfection.

CHAPTER 3

Crop in the Name of Love

Before you go skipping into a scrapbook store singing *Crop! In the Name of Love!*, stop and consider whether you are wealthy. Your answer will determine what you *need* versus what you *think you cannot live without*.

If it is any help, I am here to quell the rather humorous rumor that you need it all. Now, sure, you may find scrapbooking supplies so desirable that you *want them all*. And you may rationalize that without the latest gizmo your efficiency and your creativity will suffer overall. You may even believe you cannot live without a rotating ball-bearing disc, even though in your heart you know good and well that you most certainly do not need one. Well, do you? Frankly, I have no clue whether you do since I have no idea what a rotating ball-bearing disc does. All I know is I saw one advertised in a scrapbook magazine years ago and it looked as if it was made for some very, very serious, more-charm-than-good scrapbooking.

Speaking of serious, let us get back to the subject at hand: Scrapaholic types do love their scrapbook supplies. The only problem is that for some the love of scrapbook supplies creates repeated, albeit fleeting, greed in their lives. These normally sane individuals demonstrate restraint and dignity day in and day out until they step into a place where scrapbook supplies are sold. Then these crop shoppers can be seen rushing back and forth between the aisles, hands fluttering above their heads as they gleefully remove item after item from the dazzling display walls. Upon entering a scrapbook store, my younger sister, for one, behaves much like a squirrel madly gathering nuts—stashing little items in her check-out cart just as fast as she can. Every now and then she will suddenly stop, freeze as if she is deep in thought, then look around before scurrying off to another section, where she becomes passionate all over again and cries out that she just cannot choose. Another scrap addict told me that whenever she walks into a scrapbook store she is seized by life-affirming enthusiasm, as color, creativity, and rationalizations overwhelm her. In short, she says, she looks for discipline and finds none. Instead, she finds greed all dressed up and ready to par-tay! Dazzled, then blinded by greed, she can't see how it matters one iota if she behaves like Imelda in a shoe store. Hey, if the simile fits. Now ask yourself: Does the simile fit me? Would a metaphor suit me better?

I'm sorry that some of you may not want to hear this, but shoot—I'm just the messenger, not your husband or financial planner. Ignore the significance of what I'm saying if it makes you the least bit uncomfortable or brings up personal issues that you are currently working through. Please, however, don't attempt to return this book for a full refund. Because all kidding aside, this book should be near the top of every scrapbooker's Needs List. In fact, buy copies for all your friends who have personal issues as well.

Of course, we all realize the line between greed and need is a fine one, indeed. It is such a thin, easy-to-miss line that most of the time we don't even notice ourselves crossing it as we walk into a scrapbook store. Even I myself, normally a paragon of self-restraint [Editor: Make that self-delusion.], will never forget—at least not as long as I have my credit card debt to remind me—my first visit to a store where fine scrapbooking supplies were sold.

Years away from being a true scrapper, I thought I had my greed under control the first time I entered a scrapbooking store. I started by strolling down the aisles of beautiful decorative paper. Pass, no problem. Then I went down the album aisle. Very nice, but no thanks. Next, I found myself surrounded on both sides by row after colorful row of markers, pens, and ink pads. "Too-duh-loo!" I said, less convincingly this time, as my fingers started to twitch. Then I went around the end of an aisle and came face-to-face with hundreds of glittery, sparkling, adorably and remarkably charming embellishments. "Need pretty things!" I may have said out loud. [Editor: She did. I was standing right next to her and can swear to this.] It was that moment when the insatiable desire to have one or two of everything kicked in. Before the clerk could say "Here's a whole kit-and-cute-doodle" I was off on an acid-free spree, rushing up and down the aisle singing, "Gimme, gimme! Go, gimme!"

Soon, I had it all; everything except a good idea of what I would do with any of it. As was mentioned, I'm not yet a gifted scrapbooker.

Anyway, to put a button on it, according to a small but respected group of psychologists and a few lesser known vegetarians, scrapbooking falls under the subcategory of "Hobby," which falls under the larger category labeled "Luxury." Hard as it is to believe, in their professional opinion, scrapbooking, like a dishwasher or a trip to Barbados, is not a necessity per se. So avid scrapbookers, one could conclude, live in the Scrap of Luxury. [Editor: Let's hope there's a point to all of this.] Clearly, the point escapes me, but may in fact be found in the *Journal of Human Social Behavior*, if and when you can get your hands on a copy.

And now, moving on, we need to speak freely with one another and also consider there are no absolute rights and wrongs when it comes to making yourself happy. Please, however, keep in mind (at the back of your mind if it makes you feel better) that all we—that is to say the social behavioral scientists and I—are saying is "give *needs* a chance." Ignore your wants, make a list of your *needs*. Stick to it like spray adhesive.

Which reminds me, you need adhesive. Got to have it. Can't scrapbook without it.

CHAPTER 4

Priceless Memories

Hot flash! There comes a time in almost every scrapbooker's life when—how to say this?—a certain female discomfort of a personal nature arises, if you know what I mean. If you don't know what I mean, you're probably a man and you'd be wise to skip this chapter.

Okay, ladies. The period, as you know, comes, as a rule, at the end of the sentence. That said, and now that the men have amscrayed, let's touch on the real discomfort in your life. It's not menstruation but rather *men's frustration*, which can really cramp your scrapbooking style.

Some of you have experienced this curse firsthand—yes, we are talking about your handsome husbands, who've raised their concerns and voices when discussing the amount of money and time you spend each month on scrapbooking. Sometimes you have to wonder what the heck their problem is. I do not have to wonder since I know exactly what their problem is. (Your problem, by the way, is discussed in the previous chapter, a chapter entitled "Crop in the Name of Love.") The difficulty here with writing about *their* problem is that I am referring to a flaw in the character of the one whom you adore, and while it is understandable for you to occasionally be a tiny bit critical of the mad-as-a-hatter man you married, it just feels wrong if I join in.

So instead, for now, I will show restraint and simply share, as an example, a little anecdote about a somewhat miserly yet totally troubled individual. This man, whom I've never met and who is not married to my younger sister, is so oddly disturbed by his wife's (this is a direct quote) outrageously excessive and expensive (unquote) scrapbooking supplies that he goes around spending valuable time keeping an eye out for scrapbook embellishments that cost nothing. Which is why just the other day he cheerfully presented his wife the wad of cotton from a bottle of aspirin and said, "Here, honey, have a cloud!" Ha! What a tightwad!

A frustrated husband is among the most common causes of discomfort for a scrapbooking wife. She is bound to experience such discomfort during her periods of creating life-enhancing memory books for those she loves. (Otherwise, and for what it is worth, women commonly report positive sensations—such as relief, euphoria, invigoration, creative energy, bliss, increased or lack of appetite, and joy—during and after scrapbooking.)

What you must help your husband understand—what *you* already know in your heart—is that the value of a scrapbook has one true measure: the happiness it inspires. You know this as well as you know the back of your well-lotioned hands. The hands you use to create the scrapbooks that inspire the happiness that leads to the family's success, which adds to the pleasure that makes you so kind and keeps you from cursing the children and kicking the cat.

It goes without saying that a person who is constantly critical of *anything* having to do with scrapbooking creates far too much unnecessary tension. So if you personally have experienced uncomfortable scrutiny—criticism even—where your scrapbook purchases are concerned, here is what you must do the next time your husband complains:

(1) Be bold,

(2) look the finger-wagger in the eye, and

(3) plead the earlier-mentioned, all-important scrap of wisdom: "But sweetie, the value of a scrapbook has one true measure—the happiness it inspires!"

Now, God forbid, if your husband continues to rant and refuses to see it your way . . . well, show him the highway. Or, better yet, *you* take the high road. The most effective way of taking the high road is to grab his waistband, get a good grip, and yank his trousers out as far as they will stretch. Then, let go. When they snap back into place, shout, "Ka-ching!"

This is sure to get his attention. Once you have his attention, you can urge him to stop his whining already so everybody can just get on with life and its oh-so-important documentation.

If this fails to work, as a last retort, silence his protests by using one of these scrappy comebacks:

1. "Scrapbooking takes my mind off the stretch marks I bear as a result of carrying your children full term."

2. "If you can't say anything nice, go call your mother."

3. "Let's talk about what you just spent on your [choose one]: golf clubs; satellite dish; midlife crisis."

4. "Before you judge me, walk a mile in my shoes." [At least this gets him out of the house for a while.]

5. "Somebody needs a nap."

6. "I can't hit a man with glasses—go get me something larger and heavier."

7. "X-Y-Z!" [When he looks down to examine his zipper, run from the room.]

8. "It is either scrapbooking or we start dating other people. You choose."

9. "Nyuk! Nyuk! Nyuk!" [Follow up with a gentle two-finger poke to the eyes.]

10. "Hey! You think it's easy to visually document our lives? Well, it's not!!!" [Throw a texturing sponge at him.]

If none of these comebacks has the desired effect, try putting clouds in your ears.

CHAPTER 5

The Work of Art

Reality is overrated. This is nothing if not a good reason to escape it. Even so, when forced to face reality in all its tedium, how many among us, besides network television producers, think to bring a camera? Regrettably, too few.

Of course, this standard mistake needs correcting if you trust the philosophical experts of our day who teach that something as common and monotonous as scrubbing the bathtub or polishing the floor can inspire us, comfort us, and make us feel joyful. This sounds idiotic, I know. It does, however, support my newest notion that dull-as-dishwater events, as routine as they come, deserve to be celebrated and photographed, often and with enthusiasm.

Before scrubbing this idea out of hand, just imagine for a moment a scrapbook sparkling with photos showing you, Keeper of the House, whistling while you work. To begin, get that child (the one who follows you around all day whining that there is nothing to do) to follow you around all day with a camera as you dust, mop, sweep, sanitize, load, wax, vacuum, bleach, deodorize, wipe, unload, fold, and polish. The list is exhaustive, isn't it? Still, it is certainly no reason not to push ahead, snap on the rubber gloves, and consider the worthiness of the work behind the art while choosing one of these new and improved photo-taking plans, each of which allows you to plan your work and work your plan according to your personal preferences:[1]

    📖 **PLAN A:** Just do what you would normally do, which, I hope for your sake and sanity, would include no more than several hours' worth of clearing the clutter, wiping down the walls and floors, putting everything in its place, and strategically spraying a disinfectant around the bathroom.

    📖 **PLAN B:** Get photos showing you doing the usual cleaning plus a few extra activities such as polishing the piano keys; taking a toothbrush to the grout in the shower; and scouring the bacteria-infested, life-threatening grime at the base of the toilet in the boys' bathroom. Be sure to smile behind that protective face mask.

    📖 **PLAN C:** What do you say to making it a feng shui day? The beauty of this plan is that it's perfect for those among us who dislike the smell of harsh clean-

---

1. If you are in a position to hire others to do your housework, lucky you. Just skip along to the chapter "Put on a Happy Face."

ing products. As a scrapbooker, you likely enjoy harmony anyway, so the pictures here could show you going with the flow of energy, rearranging your lucky bamboo furniture, and dusting the Buddha in your bonsai garden. If you have the time, do include a photo of you sitting in a lotus position, levitating or something like that.

There is a **Plan D**, the never-popular Spic & Span Plan, but it involves vacuuming up the lint behind the clothes dryer—and who in her right mind gives a damn about the dust behind any major appliance? If you just said "I do!" then please, send me your address and a list of whichever prescription drugs you are taking and in return I'll send you Plan D and all of the never-been-used attachments for my deluxe vacuum.[2]

Of course, there is more to our everyday existence than housework! (Which is a relief, since otherwise I'd have no choice but to drink the cleaning fluid marked "Warning: Fatal if swallowed.") So let's not overlook these routine activities that rarely get photographed, but should: napping, cooking, flossing, clipping, combing, curling, reading, and sweeping things under the rug.

No doubt about it, excellent opportunities to capture mediocre yet meaningful memories abound. Think how much better daily life will be once we [Editor: And by "we" she means you.] take the time to give previously dull daily deeds a place of dignity in our hearts and in our scrapbooks.

2. Not a real offer.

CHAPTER 6

A Pen for Your Thoughts

There is a rumor going around, likely started by my children, that something is wrong with my brain. Now, I'm not one who goes looking for trouble, so a medical professional has not yet been consulted. Still, it wouldn't surprise me one iota if I were to wake up with a neurosurgeon standing over my opened skull shouting in disbelief, "Whoa! Somebody get a camera! There's a tumor the size of a melon in this patient's left frontal lobe!"

After recovering rapidly from the surgery, I'd begin a new life. For starters, I would wear a smaller hat. Then I would go on to help my children with difficult problems such as algebraic quantitatives and low self-esteem.

But for now my memory is nowhere near as good as it used to be, back when it was photographic. At least I assume my memory was photographic all those years ago when I was learning to speak English, my native tongue. How else could I have learned a language from scratch in such a short period of time?

But somewhere around my second or third birthday, my photographic memory started to fade. Nowadays, nobody would accuse me of having even a good memory, let alone a photographic one. Just ask my dear friend, who recently asked me the middle name of my eldest son. I gave this ordinary question some serious thought, took another sip of tea, and then confessed I could not recall the middle name of my firstborn. The more incredulous my friend became, the worse I felt. As she offered several popular boys' names as possible choices, the right answer came to me: Christopher. (Not an altogether easy name to remember, if you ask me.)

In my defense, my son Miles *Christopher* has not exactly made it easy to remember his names. When he was six years old he came home from school one day and reported his new name was Buzz. "Do not call me Miles anymore," he instructed. "If you do, I won't answer."

He wasn't kidding. His parents, along with his school teachers, were quite impressed by his unswerving ability to ignore them and anyone else who failed to call him Buzz. Meanwhile, my youngest son, Alec, whose middle name has nothing to do with any of this, idolized his older brother, Miles. In fact, he decided he wanted to be called Miles, as the name was now up for grabs. So Alec became, in name only, Miles, whereas Miles answered only to Buzz.

For a few months all was well—if weird—until Buzz (née Miles) told Alec (aka Miles) to find a new nickname and stop using Miles. Which Alec reluctantly did. Alas, all of his new trial nicknames lacked staying power. It was around then that I gave up and started calling both of my sons "Hey, you." "Hey" for short.

Back to why scrapbooking is the beloved pastime that it is, and why journaling is such an important part of scrapbooking. First, anyone in her right mind (which, as I was saying early on in this chapter, leaves me out) knows that as we age, our ability to retain information grows weaker. Everybody, sooner or later, is going to experience some memory loss. Especially those of you who have suffered one or, heaven forbid, multiple concussions.

I happen to have some experience where brain injuries and sharp blows to the head are concerned [Editor: No surprises here]; for example, the first time I blacked out was on the black-top at school when, during a spirited game of tag, I ran right into a long, taut, two-person jump rope. The last thing I remember before my head hit the ground were the words, "Apples, peaches, pears, and plums; tell me when your birthday comes! January! February! Ma . . ."—*thwack*! Next thing I know, the school nurse is standing over me holding an ice pack in one hand and a half-eaten doughnut in the other.

Years went by, and I managed to avoid any further serious head injuries. Then came the day when the side of my skull bumped into the driver's-side window during an automobile collision. Pretty serious, that injury was, but at least the accident was not my fault. The next one *was* my fault, and I just *pretended* to lose consciousness when my car rear-ended another vehicle and its driver jumped out and began shouting at me.

The next time I hit the back of my head, I was knocked out cold at an indoor ice rink. As I regained consciousness, I saw my six-year-old son had stopped skating and was offering repeated words of encouragement: "Get up, Mom, you're embarrassing me. Get up!" I was at the moment unable to get up, but had no trouble *throwing* up. With painful effort I wobbled off the ice and into the men's restroom. (That's the silver lining about head injuries; they make it so you just don't care.)

I lost consciousness only one other time and (knock on wood) that's the extent of my head injuries. Oh wait, what am I thinking? No it's not! *Ack*!, I have a terrible memory. When you lose consciousness you lose just a little bit of your ability to remember things. [Editor: And you start making the mistake of assuming everything that happens in your life is interesting and actually worth writing about. . . .] She's rude but right. Also as you grow older and suffer one head injury after another you will, in all likelihood, begin to forget particulars. Like where your car is parked, how to make instant oatmeal, and whether you ever ran with the bulls in Pamplona.

A more common and less serious problem is that you may lose your ability to name the faces from your past in your photographs. As if forgetting my son's middle name was not enough, there was also the time, not long ago, when one of my overly curious children asked about the identity of the baby in a picture he had found in the garage. Without thinking or knowing, I looked at the vaguely familiar photo and said, "I'd say that's you, darlin'!"

A few minutes later he and his brother, in the throes of simultaneous identity crises, were arguing over which of them it was in the photo. Apparently, each child had been told on separate occasions by his mother that he was the baby in the photo. Frankly, I had no clue if the baby was even mine, except that the blanket in the picture looked familiar. I was pretty sure it was one or the other of the boys, since I have only the two. I assumed it would always be easy to tell them apart because one has blue eyes and the other has brown. Unfortunately, it turns out that eye color is indistinguishable in a small, out-of-focus, fading photo that's been floating around for a good ten years.

Back to the point of this essay: Fortunately for all of us there is an easy way to improve your memory in seconds. It's called *writing everything down*. Journaling is another name for it. Scrapbookers who are good at writing down life's details are able to recall much more than your average what's-her-face.

Until the baby-photo incident I thought photographs simply spoke for themselves. At least, that was always my excuse for never writing much if anything on my pictures. Now I am careful to identify the people in my pictures. And I always write in large bold letters. You should too, because even if your photos and your memories don't fade over the years, your eyesight most surely will. (*Especially* if you ignored your mother's repeated warnings and looked directly at the sun during one of those lunar eclipses. Like Lot's wife you just *had* to look, didn't you? And now you have permanent cornea damage. Nice going. Well, what's done is done. But from here on out, always wear sunglasses, okay? And also a helmet; it never hurts to wear a helmet. Unless you are trying to get a good night's sleep.)

As a final bit of worth-taking advice, and moving on to the how-to portion of this chapter, I would like to recommend *now* as being as good a time as any to commit to memory this comprehensive list of commonsense rules about labeling and journaling in your scrapbooks:

1. **The Mighty Pen:** When journaling or labeling, always be sure to use a permanent, fade-proof,

nonbleeding, waterproof, nontoxic pen. Or, a pencil.
A pencil will do in a pinch.

2. **This Is Your Caption Speaking:** Keep in mind that
all photographs should be explained (or falsified)
by their captions.

3. **Word Play:** Jot, record, convey, note, describe, and
depict using as many words as time and space
allow. It is no longer enough to merely write down
who's who and what's what. Tell something more.
Otherwise, where's the wisdom? Where's the wit?
Where's the painstaking detail reminding you
whether you ever or never had a better time?

4. **Better Up Your Lettering:** Write legibly. If you
dislike your handwriting because, say, it looks like
that of a child or a doctor, use a computer with its
many easy-to-read fonts and special features like
Spell Cheek.

5. **Be Edgy:** Writing along the edges of your scrapbook
pages is creative and practical.

I hope you memorize these recommendations, and I wish
you the very best in your ongoing quest to keep an accurate
and organized visual and written account of your past, present, and whatever is important to you in the future. Meanwhile,
always keep your sense of humor about you. As the Termina-
tor once remarked, "Your levity is good; it relieves the fear of
death."

As for me and my future, well, as mentioned, I am having a tough time staying focused in the here and now. Which is why it will be a pleasant surprise if I can just find the energy, solitude, and wit to finish writing this chapter before I lose my, uh . . . oh, forget it—I certainly have.

CHAPTER 7

Put On
a Happy Face

A bitter truth: real life can't match scrapbook life. This is nothing if not a reason to take a good look at scrapbookers and their up-lifting tendency to commemorate the moments of their lives and the lives of those they love. Their unique way of looking at events through rose-colored lenses (now there's a cliché with a twist; feel free to use it) is particularly excellent and enviable.

Scrapbookers are the life of every pot-luck party. They laugh a lot. They say "Smile!" a lot. They use lots of exclamation points!! When they arrive, they do not simply say "Oh, hello," like a normal depressive. No, they practically shout *"Hey! Hi!! Happy to be here!!! How the heck are you?"* And before you can mut-ter "I've been better, thanks" they are laughing and slapping their thighs and saying something debatable like *"Ain't life grand!"*

Well, nothing is wrong with that, nothing at all. Only now and then it is like being talked to by a flamboyant kindergarten teacher who fails to notice you are wearing big-girl pants and underarm deodorant.

Please, ladies! Keep it down out there. Some of us are trying to weep. Some of us tend to take a bit dimmer view of existence than those of you who are always making the grass grow greener. Still, that's just me and right now I badly need some nighttime cold medicine.

Okay, we're back! Talking about scrapbookers who improve each shining moment in their quest for silver linings and everyone's good side. True scrappers picture life not entirely the way it is but the way it ought to be. Which is not to say they avoid life's woes and worries; no, like everybody, they have their hardships and their daily supply of soft drinks filled with high-fructose corn syrup, which will kill us all in the end, I'm afraid. They get rotator-cuff injuries and wounded feelings, and when they accidentally cut themselves with an X-acto knife—yes, they bleed.

All of which forces them to wipe tears from their faces one cheek at a time like everybody else.

Really, is there a scrapbooker alive who has not experienced holiday weight gain, nonathletic children with athlete's foot, noticeable loss of upper-arm muscle tone, hair, or husband? (There is? Is it you? Well, either you are very young or very lucky and you should keep it to yourself or something as large as life will come over there and give you something to cry about.)

The important and remarkable thing is that scrapbookers know life is rife with strife, yet they continually go out of their way to focus on what's so good about it. They are not about denial; they are about as optimistic as a person can be. It helps that they spend so much time pursuing an activity that kindles inspiration, friendships, and memories. It reminds them of what is truly valuable.

For example, take the devoted scrapper who recently put an enormous amount of effort and time into organizing what she hoped would be a joyous birthday party for her five-year-old twins. The party turned out to be a disaster in anyone's book—except this mother's scrapbook, which ended up including photo after photo of ideal party images. The unpleasant moments were excluded because, after all, in the final analysis, who wants to see photos of panic-stricken party guests refusing to sit on a pony? Or swashbuckling guests splattering ketchup and mustard as they dueled it out with their lunch entrees? And nobody I know personally would enjoy reliving the scene where a tot playfully pushed a coin so far up his nose that his mother, after making matters worse by trying to remove the foreign object herself ("Blow! Blow! No! You're sniffing! I said 'Blow'!!") had no choice but to promptly head for the doctor's office.

In any event, life conspires to remind us that even the best of times can turn on a dime. Some events are not meant to be captured on film, which is why none of the unpleasant or haphazard party moments made it into the scrapbook. Out of sight, out of mind. A mother's wish for a happy birthday came true, if only on the pages of her scrapbook.

So hats off to scrapbookers and their sunny ways of taking lemons and making (pictures of) lemonade. Their creativity comes from the heart, and it goes to the heart of what makes them so extraordinary. Even when life is perfectly peccant [Editor: She claims to have looked it up; supposedly, it means "bad."] scrapbookers will slap on a happy face and spread sunshine all over the page. And that's why, in truth, I LOVE THEM SO MUCH!!!

CHAPTER 8

Fancy Pants

It is true: I have never met a scrapbooker I did not like. Except for the one who recently sat across the aisle from me on a four-hour flight.

A flouncy-haired woman, she pretentiously placed a carry-on across her lap, looked around to see if everyone was watching, flicked her wrist, and *shebang*! Her tote sprung up and out, turning into a scrapbooker's deluxe workstation—complete with cutting board, paper-making kit, and Handi Wipes.

Looking extremely pleased with herself, she smiled down at a vast selection of papers, neatly organized in see-through pockets and snap-lock closures, accompanied by archival dividers and everything else a scrapbooker could dream of, including that famous rotating ball-bearing disc. Meanwhile, I had lost my bearings, envious as I was of her extravagant show of templates, pads, border stickers, and pages-in-progress.

With a self-satisfied glance in my direction, this serious scrapper repeatedly rubbed her thumbs back and forth across the tips of her fingers before grabbing some colored pens from their loops and cutting loose. As the stamping and cutting and cropping got going, this scrapper began chanting under her breath, "Like this . . . like that . . . like this, this, this! . . . Like that!" All the while her elaborate charm bracelet, dangling everything from miniature silver scissors (how she ever got past airport security with those is anyone's guess) to tiny framed photos, clattered and jangled like a janitor's keys.

During the entire flight, she demonstrated this rapid way of cropping, pausing only once to thoughtfully ponder a page. After what seemed like forever, she snapped her fingers in that way that says, "Look at me! I'm a flamenco dancer!" then sequentially yanked a dozen or so little charms from her bracelet and glued them, just like that, into her scrapbook. "Ah, well, no *charm* done," she said, laughing at her senseless pun.

"Au *contraire*! More charm than good!" I said, but my corrective pun was muffled by the in-flight pillow I'd placed against my face before responding.

By the time the flight captain's voice asked the crew to prepare for landing, this woman had finished her scrapbook and put away her workstation, and was brushing gold glitter from her augmented chest. Smiling, she accepted the compliments and extra bags of peanuts from the flight attendants who seemed genuinely awed by the scrapbooking skills of Miss Fancy Pants. It was a relief, let me tell you, to be taking my leave from this exceedingly accomplished scrapbooker around whom I had the heavy heart of a have-not.

So anyhoo, I was feeling deprived—call it peanuts envy—as

I exited the plane and headed in the direction of the airport's baggage claim. I am one of those people who can't walk and feel glum at the same time, so I tried instead to cheerfully sashay. It was no use. Then all of sudden, fate threw me a bone. Unexpectedly, I saw something that lifted my spirits, lightened my load, and made me wish I had a camera. There she was, Miss You-Know-Who, waltzing along as if she owned the place, totally unaware that a wide self-adhesive border, all shiny and blue, was stuck to her rear, wagging like a tail.

It was so funny I forgot to laugh quietly.

As a rule, I am not envious of another's good fortune or superior talents since that would be both wrong and time-consuming. Yet at that moment it felt good to tell myself that even though I did not have her charmed life or her deluxe scrapbooking workstation, neither did I have a sparkly sticker stuck to my bottom.

CHAPTER 9

True Scrapper

Now let's say for the sake of creating another chapter for this book, you are but one of the many artistic do-it-yourselfers out there who wonders if (even hopes that) you have what it takes to become a true scrapper, aka a 35mm Mama, Scrapaholic, Queen Cropper, Memory Keeper, Photo Fiend, or Stampaholic.

Well, your chances of becoming a true scrapper are more or less 50/50 if you are a female living in North America and you own a camera. The odds in your favor increase dramatically if you are a multitasker who has repeatedly demonstrated loose-limbed energy, an eye for color, and the ability to load a Nikon while holding a cell phone and driving a minivan. Also, but not always, your prospects improve significantly if your parents gave you a perfectly good name at your birth, which you have managed to perk up by adding a "y" to its ending or altering it completely to better fit your upbeat personality.

If any of the above remind you of yourself, go grab your photos, missy—you are well on your way to becoming a raging Scrapaholic. To be certain, review and thoughtfully consider these frequently asked questions and answers, most of which were made up:

Q: Is taking a lot of pictures the first sign I am turning into a Scrapaholic?

A: Heck no! Plenty of people take plenty of pictures but never get around to getting their film developed. These people are slothaholics, but that's another chapter, the one where I share my personal habits.

Q. Can Scrapaholics be cured?

A. Yes, if you live in Never-never land. Otherwise, there is no such thing as a recovering scrapaholic. And as I explained in Chapter 1, there's no such thing as Scrapaholics Anonymous since anonymity is the furthest thing from a scrapbooker's mind. There are times, for example, say, during a bout of giving birth to a baby or a stint as PTA president, when a scrapbooker may step back from her obsession, but the various support groups are always there to get her scrapping back on track.

Q. What about sobriety?

A. You must mean sorority, sister! Many scrapbookers join scrapper groups such as the Happy Scrappers, Teeny Croppers, Cutting-edgers, Grass Croppers, Memorabilia Maniacs, City Stickers, and Women Who Run with Scissors.

Q. Are specific groups of people more likely to become Scrapaholics?

A. A good question, if a redundant one. Scrapaholism cuts across race and even nationality. In fact, Scrapaholics cut across anything they think might look good in a scrapbook. In general, though, more women than men experience insatiable scrapbooking needs and seem to have healthier and more active scrap drives than men.

Q. Is owning more than one holiday-themed sweater a sign I may be a true scrapper?

A. Yes, and duh.

Now, before you go off half-cropped and purchase lots of scrapbook supplies, just hold your hobbyhorses. Stop and consider the warning signs below and accept the fact that obsessive scrapbooking is not for everybody. Sad to say, your chances of becoming a truly talented scrapbooker are slim if:

1. You often use profanity in front of your children, and vice versa.

2. Your most recent photo was taken in a police station.

3. The only pictures you have of your children were taken on Photo Day at their school.

4. You are me.

5. Your year-old disposable camera has exposures remaining.

6. Your mother wears army boots.

7. You don't know the words to the theme song from the movie *The Way We Were*.

8. Your children's birthday invitations go out the day before the event via the telephone.

9. Your only layout idea requires SPF 30 sunblock.

10. You never bother to remove your film from your luggage before sending it through airport security.

11. You use photographs of your family members as drink coasters.

12. You think this is a book written by a fool who is full of sound and flurry but without a lick of sense.

CHAPTER 10

Tips for New Scrapbookers

So you want to create a scrapbook? For the life of me, I can't think of a better thing to do in your spare time. It certainly beats sitting around doing what I often do, which is try to solve the mysteries of the universe. [Editor: She has yet to figure out where her paycheck goes.] Hard as it is to believe, there remains a substantial, albeit rapidly shrinking, group of us who have yet to join the ranks of *successful* scrapbookers. For me, I swear [Editor: and how], scrapbooking is one artistic struggle after another. Still, you must live and learn and never give up, even if you are trying to create a scrapbook that is as extraordinary as the ones you keep coming across in the homes of experienced scrapbookers.

Despite what I just said, it is fairly easy to create a scrapbook. It is easy and enjoyable once you make the commitment. Some may say it is all in the wrist, but as far as I am concerned it is all in the commitment. It is also in the doing, of course, the actual scrapbooking, but that still leaves a lot of it in the commitment—even though some will go to their graves *insisting* it's all in the wrist. So if you are ready to be committed, ready to jump in with both feet, then I envy you and I applaud you. Also, I have a little start-up advice for you. [Editor: Better yet, reader, skip this chapter altogether. In fact, a much more productive use of your time would include banging your head against the wall.]

In an effort to give you the best possible advice, I spoke briefly with my sisters, two of whom are highly skilled, truly gifted, contest-winning makers of memory books. They provided some excellent tips and I thought up some more on my own, so you can be pretty darn confident that what you are about to read is as good as it gets, scrapbook-advice wise. [Editor: Uh, don't bet on it. I've seen her most recent attempt at scrapbooking and it was good only for a few laughs. By the way, didn't I tell you to skip this chapter?]

Pay no attention to that woman behind the curtain. Who cares, really, that I'm no scrapbook professional? Nobody here! Still, to avoid any misunderstanding or lawsuits it should be revealed, once and for all, that I am not now nor have I ever been qualified to give step-by-step advice—or any advice, for that matter—when it comes to layout, layering, or lettering. The essential thing is I know a good scrapbook when I see it, and as far as I can tell a good scrapbook starts with good photos.

Ha ha! You know, of course, that that was a joke. Photos are the *least* of your concerns when it comes to creating a good scrapbook page. Still, you are going to encounter a tiny snag without some pictures on hand, so I suggest you run out and take some photos of people you know fairly well. Enough to create a social record of this time in your life, in the life of your family, or in the life of your friends. If you are currently without family and friends (and who isn't at times?) and dislike having your own picture taken, don't feel so bad. There is also great satisfaction in taking pictures of your favorite things.

Visually speaking, these are a few of my personal favorite things. (But you go right ahead and photograph them for yourself. I don't mind; in fact I'd be happy for you.) They are: whiskers, kittens, kettles made from bright copper, packages in brown paper and secured with mailing tape (I prefer string-tied packages, but the U.S. Postal Service does not), and winters that are so white they appear to be silver (wear woolen mittens if you plan to photograph this one).

The next bit of scrapbooking advice is this: Become familiar with the many scrapbook supplies out there. This is sure to take you the better part of all the spare time remaining in your life, but it will be worth it. I recommend daily trips to a nearby scrapbook store, where you will find everything from colored cardstock to quick-drying photo glue to an unfettered feeling of lightheartedness—every single thing you need to create your first scrapbook, except artistic talent.

If you lack artistic talent, no sweat—as long as you follow this next tip: Take a scrapbooking class. Part technique instruction, part bonding ritual, this beloved gathering for women is the biggest trend since Bunko & Botox parties. Scrapbooking classes will teach you how to tell good crops from bad crops; decoupage from appliqué, and Michele Gerbrandt from Lisa Bearnson. It's also where you will find yourself sitting around a table with other scrapbook enthusiasts and their cherished photos and supplies. As a beginner you must resist the urge to compare your children or your creativity to other scrapbookers', unless you want to slink out and drive home in a state of agonized insecurity and self-doubt.

Another temptation you must avoid is the one where you "borrow" another person's photographs or page-layout ideas without first asking permission. Remember, scrappers have sharp tools and they are not afraid to use them.

The last valuable directive is a familiar but often ignored three-word bit of advice: Less is more. For financial as well as aesthetic reasons, limit the number of decorative items you include on any given scrapbook page. While there is nothing wrong with using, say, a two-dimensional title strip on patterned cardstock surrounded by embossed lettering, some fancy stitching, and a few buttons, you should draw the line when you get so much on there you don't have room for the photo. If your enthusiasm for embellishments leaves your page looking like something out of *Where's Waldo?*, consider drawing a big, bold arrow directing the eye to the photo. Your friends and loved ones will thank you.

Well, I'm whipped, so I'll leave you with these last scraps of wisdom: Be quirky, be clever, and just be yourself rather than somebody else. It'll save you time and confusion in the long run.

One more thing? If you try and fail, as I have done on occasion, to create a great scrapbook, you can always try again in the future. Meantime, study carefully the scraps of wisdom in this book. They may help you better understand scrapbooking and the astonishing role it plays in other people's lives. Also, if it helps, take comfort in the fact that nearly half of the people on the face of the Earth will never be great scrapbookers—yet they can still lead perfectly happy lives. Lives that their wives document with picture-perfect scrapbooks.

Author's note: This chapter is over, so you should feel free to turn the page and begin a new one, unless you want to stay around and learn the words to a lively scrapbooking song. This can be sung to the tune of "My Favorite Things" from the popular movie *The Sound of Music*, which, if you've never seen it, do! It's a pretty great film with many likeable and memorable characters, especially the nuns and one nun in particular.

My Favorite *Scrapbooking* Things

Stamping and cropping and colorful blocking,
Layouts and eyelets and whimsical chalking,
Photo reminders of joys that life brings,
These are a few of my scrapbooking things.
When the spouse barks, when the kids whine,
When my hair looks bad,
I simply assemble a wonderful page
And then I don't feel so bad.
[Editor: You already used "bad."] [Author: So?]

So, dyeing and glossing and late-night embossing,
Stitching and bitching and bad-idea tossing,

Journaling meant to remind me of things,
These are a slew of my scrapbooking blings!

When the dog barks, when the kids bite,
When I need time that's sweet
I simply assemble a beautiful page
And then I just tap my feat!

CHAPTER 11

Everybody Smile

A couple of years ago, all of the children in my extended family
went over the river and around the bend to their grandmother's
house, where a group photograph of the grandchildren was to
be taken. Everybody who is anybody in the family was there.

You can always tell who belongs to which specific family
unit by the colors in their hair, the clothes they wear, whether
they play the piano well, and the language they use. This is why
some of us, in an attempt to blend in at family gatherings, issue
last-minute reminders and warnings regarding etiquette and ac-
ceptable behavior before allowing our children to get out of the
car. The reminders will always start off with something like,
"Okay, everybody, remember—behave yourselves!" Or:

> **PARENT:** Time to review the rules: One! Stay away from
> grandma's piano.

CHILD: (whining) But I just learned a new Japanese song called Chopsticks!

PARENT: No, not a chop, not a stick.

CHILD: Today is opposite day, so . . .

PARENT: Rule number two: No armpit noises, burping, or repeating everything your brother says.

CHILD: Repeating everything your brother says.

PARENT: THREE! Never ask a person if she is going to have a baby.

CHILD: Why?

PARENT: It's rude.

CHILD: (patting his mother's stomach) Are you going to have a baby?

PARENT: Four! Whatever you do, which better be nothing, remember: Absolutely no goofing off when the time comes to have your picture taken with your cousins. No crossed eyes, pig noses, or tongues sticking out.

CHILD: (touching the tip of his tongue to the tip of his nose) 'Ou 'een 'ike 'is?

My lovely older sister is a high-strung, highly organized scrapbooking freak who, and I really must hand it to her here, certainly knows how to organize an event. Weeks before, she had contacted everybody and suggested (which is to say, insisted) that every child wear a red, blue, or yellow brand-specific polo shirt and khakis. She emphasized *clean* khakis when speaking to some of us. Thus unsoiled, we all arrived and soon the photographer was setting up his camera gear and parents were arranging their children according to shirt color, height, and how well-groomed they were. The boys and girls with scrapbooking moms were used to this type of set-up situation, since their world is a staged one. Naturally, they behaved nicely. Some of the other children—the more free-spirited ones, we'll say—despite being forewarned in the car, were less able to cooperate because they were too busy repeating everything the photographer said.

One particular child [Editor: A child who is a spitting image of the author.] behaved so badly his mother felt the need to laugh nervously and remind everyone how from the get-go this kid had been unlucky when it came to having his picture taken. She went on to explain how the photographs from the first moments of this child's life had been ruined. "So eager was I to see my baby's birth photos; so anxious to relive the birth process, which, by the way, had me in stitches—more stitches than you can count [Editor: Right here is where she lost her male listening audience.]; so excited to see my new child in pictures, that I found myself at the photo lab counter just days after the delivery. There I stood, cradling a newborn, when instead of photographs I'm handed—you will not believe this—a typewritten note of apology explaining how my film had been destroyed—destroyed!—during the developing process. Can you believe it? I couldn't believe it! I simply would not believe it if I hadn't NOT seen the photographs for myself! No mother should have this happen to her! There was hysteria in my voice when I asked that photo-processing clerk to please explain how one recaptures on film the crowning, the birthing, the cutting of the umbilical cord? Exactly how, I wanted to know, was I supposed to re-create that once-in-a-lifetime event? Well, the clerk, he couldn't say, he just repeated his weak apologies in a louder voice so as to be heard above the wails of my baby."

CHAPTER 12

Man-Made Scrapbooks

Have you ever, ever, ever in your short-lived life seen a scrapbooking husband with his scrapbooking wife? I have, but it was court ordered, I'm pretty sure.

Rare are the scrapbooking men. Why is that? For starters, scrapbooking is a fundamental law of nurture, and women by nature are more nurturing. This may be a lie, but I don't think so. One woman I know went so far as to claim she is more nurturing than any man alive, now that Mr. Rogers, God bless him, is no longer with us.

Still, as we all know, there are a tremendous number of extremely nurturing men out there. One can hardly ignore the fact that nowadays nearly half of the people pushing strollers and planting flower gardens are males. At least in my neighborhood, where most of the women ran off after claiming their husbands were unkind and uncaring.

I am kidding, of course. None of the men in my neighborhood plant flower gardens.

Anyway, to be fair—since we are the fairer sex—let us allow the possibility that men are just as nurturing as women and consider some other conceivable reasons why so few males, relatively speaking, are scrapbookers. Your guess is as good as mine, but my guess is: big hands. Not many men attend crop parties because their hands are, as a rule of thumb, too large to scrapbook comfortably. As anyone who's ever picked up a grommet or a pop-dot can tell you, many scrapbooking tools and embellishments are made for people whose hands are smaller than those found below the wrists of your average male. What the scrapbooking industry needs if it's going to attract more men is an innovative set of tools for people who can palm a basketball.

On the other hand, Palm Pilots and cell phones have buttons no bigger than the exclamation point at the end of this sentence and men have no trouble using these devices! So perhaps the real reason more guys don't scrapbook is that persons with big hands are not big on *themes*. It seems to me theme parties are partly to blame for the lack of scrapbooking males. What man, unless he was legally drunk, would wear his favorite pajamas to a social gathering? What man, really, even admits to having a favorite pair of pajamas? Scrapper Girls just want to have fun. Scrapper Boys, on the contrary, do not. At least not when the fun involves putting on fuzzy slippers and doing the Bunny Crop around the room.

I, for one, would not be the least bit startled to learn there are plenty of wonderful husbands, sons, and fathers out there who greatly enjoy scrapbooking in the privacy of their own homes.

Chances are, they can emboss, punch, and stamp with the best of them. Still, they would not refer to themselves as "Happy Scrappers," nor would they like it one iota if either you or I referred to them as such. We could call them Male Scrappers but for the fact it sounds too Chippendale-ish.

Call them what you will, but don't ever call on male scrapbookers to publicly wear a T-shirt that is too cute for words, i.e., a T-shirt sporting the words, "I ♥ to scrap." Personally, and I feel strongly about this, I think advertising anything, from your personal opinion to a company's emblem, on any item of clothing is a bad idea unless you are being handsomely paid for it. Pictures and words have their place, but it is not on my back or across your chest. It clutters up your personal space, not to mention the aesthetics of the world at large. Just this morning I saw a woman wearing no fewer than seven different logos. Everything from her baseball cap to her handbag bore company logos, companies that had no doubt charged her extra money to advertise for them. That is why, if you live under my roof, you are forbidden to wear clothing with pictures or words, except in the rarest of situations. Say, for example, you are a member of a little league baseball team and are required to wear a uniform, or . . . [Editor: Excuse us a minute while I talk to her about ranting.]

Then again, who am I to say what anyone else should wear or should not wear? Live and let live, my sister is always telling me. What's more, we have other important things to consider—such as whether you are a man, a man who is now concerned because you are a scrapbooker or you were thinking about taking up scrapbooking but are now concerned that if you do others may think you have small hands for a guy. So for the sake of setting the record straight and alleviating fears, let me be clear: I certainly do not know what men who scrapbook are about, except that they are unlikely to show up at an all-night crop party wearing pajamas. That I know—but that's all I know.

CHAPTER 13

Fabric of Society

The sewing room was in the basement. Its door was always open, yet it was the one room in the house where my mother was able to find solitude. A cozy, warm (think sauna), brick-walled, windowless place, it was frequently filled with the humid aroma of laundry detergent, fabric softener, and freshly ironed cotton. Wicker baskets piled high with folded clothes lined a long shelf above an equally long table that seemed always to be covered with towels that needed folding and table-cloths that needed to be pressed. Although the room was primarily used for washing, drying, and ironing chores, it was called the sewing room because it was where Mother would sit at her silver Singer machine and stitch up a storm.

The original material girl, Mom made her children's clothing from fabric purchased by the bolt, which meant our outfits often matched as we marched through life like the von Trapp family singers, only without the curtain calls. It was a give/give situation: We gave our mother time alone and she gave us apparel. Except for the plaid culottes, it worked out just fine.

Recently, our mother questioned the wisdom of any woman devoting an entire room of her home to scrapbooking. My sister (who has devoted an entire room of her home to scrapbooking) was quick to point out that as far as benefiting the family, scrapping is today what sewing was back then. "One could say," I said, "you were a seamstress; your daughter is a scrapstress. Same thing."

This comparison made Mother clap her hands to her chest in a way that made me worry she needed CPR until I realized she was simply having an emotional spasm.

"If you think sewing was the joyful activity scrapbooking is," she said, "you're wrongeddy, wrong, wrong!

"Mind you," she went on, "children must be fed and clothed—everything else is lotsa la-tee-dah!" Silently she aimed her pointer finger at each of us. "Not one of you ever had a fancy photo album growing up, yet all of you turned out just fine in my book!" (Painful pause.) "So? So what if you're not the lead story on the society page, at least you all have your clothes under control."

This from a woman wearing plaid culottes and flip-flops.

Our sister, never one to just let it ride, said, "Oh, *c'mon*! Think about it, Mother—scrapbooking, just like sewing, requires creativity, material, scissors, and sacrifice. Today, a child without a scrapbook feels about as well-loved as a child with nothing but hand-me-downs."

As an adult whose children don't yet have decent scrapbooks but who do on occasion wear hand-me-downs, I was about to protest before my sister put her hands out, palms up, and shifted them up and down as if she were weighing some extremely vital yet totally invisible comparison: "Sewing, scrapbooking," she said, "sewing, scrapbooking—both contribute to the fabric of society."

All of this our mother wisely considered while holding her elbow in one hand and rubbing her chin with the other. "Good," she said. "Now you know how I felt." Which made no sense as far as it goes, yet it is her most often used nonsequitur comeback, next to, "Sharper than a serpent's tooth."

Concerned that our mother's memories of happy times spent in her sewing room were fading like cheap cotton in the spin cycle, we started bringing up all sorts of fond reminiscences. It was befitting, for instance, for one sister to recall how we each used to stand as motionless as possible on the sturdy sewing chair, chatting away while Mom, with straight pins clamped between her lips, made comforting muffled responses to show she was listening as she marked the hemlines of our skirts Just Above the Knee and No Higher Young Lady. One sister recalled the giddy anticipation she experienced when Mother picked up her heavy, saw-toothed sewing scissors and started snipping through the layers of cloth carefully pinned to tissue-paper patterns laid out on the sewing table. We all agreed there was a special feeling knowing our hand-*tailored* clothes were one-of-a-kind originals made from patterns and buttons we had purchased for ourselves from the House of Fabric.

Then, to keep the good memories rolling, we had a laugh at my recollection from long ago of the trousers our mother had made without using a pattern or measurements. After I went to her with a tearful, late-night plea for new pants to wear on a school field trip the next day, she told me not to fret, she would whip something up. In the early morning, my sleep-deprived mother sewed on a button, bit off a thread, then turned to press the seams flat with her steam iron just minutes before I ran out the door to catch the school bus—clad in a new pair of black slacks that fit like a glove. Literally—they looked like dance tights with a big, poufy crotch, which is why I was able to wear them only once and why a third-grade classmate nicknamed me Spider Legs.

It seemed fitting and was comforting to sit around and share recollections of the more traditional items our mother's loving hands had made: frilly Easter dresses with decorative eyelet lace and matching hair bows; flannel nightgowns presented every Christmas Eve; plaid school jumpers; Halloween costumes worn with store-bought plastic masks that never failed to smell toxic.

We spent the better part of an hour chit-chatting happily, looking back at what an important part of our identity was sewn up in that little room in our childhood home. As Mother dabbed a few tears of joy from her rosy cheeks and chuckled, "Spider legs!" one of us, as a final thought, said her fondest memory had to be the one of Mom cheerfully knitting us those slippers with the big pom-poms. We all smiled and nodded up and down . . . except for our mom, who shook her head left to right and sadly said, "That must have been somebody else's mother— I never learned to knit. Or purl, for that matter."

Ah, scraps! Scraps from the past, like a book filled with photos, can trigger all sorts of revisions to family memories.

CHAPTER 14

A Scrapbooking Room of One's Own

To paraphrase Virginia Woolf: To be a scrapbooker, one must have money and a room of one's own.

I suppose it goes without saying that a room of one's own does not necessarily mean an actual "room" with, say, a ceiling, four walls, large windows, natural light, gorgeous views, nice furniture, posh rugs, a ventilating system, a craftsman-quality organizational pantry, a door that locks, a surround-sound stereo system, and more storage space than a small scrapbook-supply store. No, a room of your own could just as easily and far more likely be a designated room-y *area* of your own; a quiet place with a flat surface and space to store your rotating ball-bearing disc. (If you actually have a scrapbook room that resembles the one described above, congratulations on having more money than God.)

Like most of us, when you start off on your scrapbooking

adventures, chances are you won't have a spare table, let alone a spare room—so you must go about creating one. A resourceful friend, whom I greatly admire, did this very thing the day she made the commitment to become a serious scrapper. After looking around her house for a place where she could create scrapbooks without constant interruption, she chose the dining room. She chose this spacious room for its existing coordinated color scheme, lovely accents, fine fabrics, patterned paper on the walls, accessories, sterling silver tools, and a surface so flat and clean you could eat off of it. Before anyone in her family could dish out complaints, she unloaded nearly two decades' worth of photos from large storage containers bearing the names of members of her family, covering the spacious mahogany table (a table that up until then had been nothing but a gathering place for loved ones to enjoy meals on Sundays, birthdays, and major holidays) and shouted, "Whooooeee!"

That was over a year and many completed albums ago. She's been scrapbooking in the dining room, and her family has been eating in the breakfast nook, ever since. A small inconvenience, if you ask me. Ask her husband and he'll just turn and walk out of the room balancing his dinner plate on his Golf Scrapbook. I asked one of her three teenage children what she thought of the pile of photos and scrapbook supplies taking up all the space in the dining room, and she asked right back, "You talkin' to me?"

When I assured her I was indeed talking to her and repeated my question, she communicated her great appreciation and admiration for her mother's scrapbooking tenacity by shrugging. When I encouraged her to expound, she said, "Mom hasn't done anything this outstanding, this brilliant, this, dare I say, life-changing, since she taught me to ride a bicycle." (At least I think that is what she said—either that or she asked, "You still talkin' to me?")

Another woman I know and greatly admire started off creating scrapbooks late at night on her kitchen table. This lasted maybe a month. See, her husband is a late-night eater and her baby is a late-night feeder—so soon photos were showing signs of formula and food damage. Besides which, her kitchen table always had an unpleasant adhesive quality, residue from honey, syrup, and whatever other sticky foods were used in the course of a day. So she moved all of her scrapbooking supplies into her bedroom, where she could just let things lie during the day and work on scrapbooking page projects at night. Sure, it took away much of the romantic ambience that had before permeated that little boudoir, but life is a trade-off, don't we all know, and she claims the bedroom has become the idyllic place for her to conceive scrapbook page ideas.

Then there is the example of the woman I know whose scrapbooking addiction led her to tell her own son to move out. "My scrapbooking began as an idle pursuit; a way to pass the time pleasantly and to reminisce; to capture a life of memories, if you will," she explained. "Yet straightaway, I began to scrapbook in earnest, so it wasn't long before I had patterned papers stacked as high as an elephant's eye. That's when I felt I must have a room of my own in this house; an entity unto itself, away from my husband, who has started repeating himself all the time."

"That's funny," I interjected, "because lately I've been repeating *myself* all the time. It all began, oh, let me see, when—"

"That's nice dear, so anyway, please stop interrupting," she said before continuing. "As I was saying, no matter what, I was going to have my own room, so—and I had no choice here—I told my son to move out. 'Go back to school! Get a haircut! Stand up straight, I need your room,' I told him," she said.

"That boy! He claimed he would never forgive me for kicking him out, but ha! He has, and furthermore, he married his piano teacher, who was also nearly fifty years old," she added bemusedly.

When asked if she had any advice for younger scrapbookers, she said, "Yes: Go back to school, get a haircut, stand up straight, and get a room of your own."

So let me conclude by saying that women, young and old alike, must have their own scrapbooking space. So go forward, forge every dream, but be patient and remember what one scrapbooker who has created a nice scrapbooking room of her own told me, "My Room wasn't built in a day."

To which I replied, "A bad pun, like a bad perm, is the lowest form of humor."

Scrap Depot

Take it from me: A wing nut, round-ended pliers, a hammer, a pint-sized paper piercer, and decorative scissors in your scrapbooking tool kit are, sorry to say, no longer going to cut it. The tool kit, in fact, is being replaced by tool chests, tool benches, even tool *sheds*, depending on individual scrapbookers' storage needs.

When it comes to creating some of today's trendier scrapbook page designs, the serious scrapbookers among us are venturing into areas traditionally considered bastions for the sorts of people who spit in public and grow patches of hair on their chests. Yes, the more adventurous scrapbookers are now carving out their own niches in their husbands' workshops and shopping in the aisles of the local hardware stores.

Not so long ago, for example, my friend called and woke me

at the crack of dawn to see if I wanted to go with her to Home Depot. It was an emergency—she was desperate to get her hands on a good crop saw and a narrow-belt sander. I reminded her it was Christmas Day and Home Depot would be closed. "Oy!" she said, then asked, "Do you think the Gas 'n' Go Food Mart sells tools?"

They did not. So the next day I went with this scrapbooking friend who so badly needed a crop saw and narrow-belt sander, and watched in silence as she stood riveted by the selection of zinc-plated steel tools. Finally, she filled her orange, man-sized shopping cart with all the implements, including safety goggles, she felt sure she would need to complete an advanced page lay-out. She encouraged me to treat myself to some tools, but see-ing as I am new to scrapbooking and was not anywhere near ready for a crop saw, I declined. She did, however, convince me to purchase an assortment of pipe cleaners, which are not, as their name suggests, actually used for cleaning pipes.

While I am clearly not the person to predict the future of scrapbooking, I venture to guess it will not include more pipe cleaners and will include a whole lot more industrial-size tools. As luck would have it, some of the tools you will need are as close as your garage. If you don't care to spend all the money necessary to complete your new scrapbooking tool set, you can always go into your husband's workshop area and borrow his. While you're at it, borrow his Swiss Army Knife. This little gem is a must-have item! I always carry one in my purse for emergencies, like the time, for ex-ample, my son refused to sit still in church. Exasperated, I finally just gave him my knife to keep him occupied. (He confessed later to carving "I am bored" into the pew, so now I must think twice about giving him a blade in any place of worship.)

Anyway, as for your husband's tools, take what you want. I've never met a man who isn't happy to let his wife borrow his tools. "Mi hacksaw es tu hacksaw" they will say when you ask to borrow a hacksaw. As long as you ask before taking a tool and as long as you put the tool back unbroken, just as you found it, the situation will ultimately be one of sharing and mutual respect. If, however, you are careless with his tools, he will take them with him when he leaves you for good.

Having recently spent the better part of an hour surrounded by aisles of tools, I have a few big ideas for ways existing tools might be tweaked and slightly altered to make them highly useful to scrapbookers. By all means, feel free to run with these tool ideas—if not with the tools themselves.

Empowering Tools

CROP SAW: See it, saw it! A cute crop saw to see you through scrapbook projects that require cutting up, cutting out, or cutting through. Also, crop saws are used for your basic cuts and your cuts requiring basic stitches.

SCRAP SNAP STRAP: An easy-to-snap strap that used properly will guarantee photographs, die-cuts, and small children stay put. These will be specially designed for photo framework and matting. Also, may prove ideal for hilarious practical jokes at scrapbook retreats.

NARROW-BELT SANDER: Get into the loops! Available in black or brown, these lovely sanding belts not only complement any pair of slacks but are made to smooth or distress the surface of many a scrapbooking embellishment. Also good for exfoliating dry, dull skin cells around your midsection.

MAGNIFYING GLASS: You will have it made in the shade with this convex lens tool designed to singe cardstock in decorative ways when combined with the hot ultraviolet rays of the sun. When held up to old group photos, this tool can also be useful in identifying people with extra-small heads.

SCRAP STAPLER: This precious little tool will drive and secure prong-style staples. Caution: If used improperly, it will attach your entire scrapbook to your table. Truly perfect, however, for installing felt, fabric, carpeting, roofing, and insulation.

DREAM DRILL: Designed to become the most popular scrapbooking tool ever, the dream drill will bore holes, drive screws and brads, attach hinges, brush away chalk, sand edges, mix paint, and stir the imagination.

SQUEEZE CLAMPS: Light-duty clamps designed with a repeat squeeze handle. Good for performing the scrapbooking exercises recommended by Dr. Kegel.

THE COMMON QUARTER: Two bits, four bits, six bits, a dollar, all for this common household item stand up and holler! A twenty-five-cent piece will help you make quick scrapbooking decisions when it comes to choosing colors, patterns, die-cuts, fonts, whatever! Just flip the coin; heads or tails, you always come up a winner.

Tools for Mass Page Deconstruction

CROP CHISEL: This chisel helps you out of a tight crop. It features a harpoon-like tip perfect for light cutting on cardstock and scratching hard-to-reach areas such as that place just to the left of the middle of your back.

NAIL PULLER: A notch designed for removing brads from pages or bread from toasters, if and only if, the toaster is neither plugged into an electrical socket nor submerged in water. Limited quantity available in pink.

CROPPER'S CROWBAR: Cock-a-doodle-doo! Crow all you want with this curved tool that easily fits behind photographs or between two children who need separation. The long handle provides leverage to pry photos or people apart.

RIP SAW: A dainty little saw used to buzz along after you yell, "Let 'er rip!"

Well! Tool-dee-doo! Happy scrapping to you! Love your hair, hope you win! [Editor: This is what she always says when she can think of nothing coherent to say.]

C H A P T E R   1 6

To Scrap or Not to Scrap?

You English majors and lovers of the world's greatest author may be hoping this chapter is an introduction to a Shakespearean style of scrapbooking. Alas, dear reader, 'tis not. 'Tis nuttin' more than an uninspired decision to take the oft overused "to be or not to be" line and throw it up there as a chapter title.

Nonetheless, as a chapter title it is not without relevance. You see, "To scrap or not to scrap" is in fact the very question one must repeatedly and audibly ask oneself, unless one is riding on public transportation while eating cereal straight from the box. (Interesting side note: I actually witnessed a neatly coifed, smartly dressed middle-aged woman in a subway car talking loudly to herself while rapidly eating fistfuls of Cocoa Puffs straight from the box, no milk. It was many years ago, so I don't recall what it was she was saying, but it might have been "I will not talk to myself, I will not talk to myself!" It is safe to say it was not, "I'm cuckoo for Cocoa Puffs, cuckoo for Cocoa Puffs!" Now that I am an older and wiser citizen of the world I would be less stunned and, I hope, more compassionate. Today, if I saw a person going on about something and spewing bits of dry cereal in public, I would be more likely to lean over and whisper to my traveling companions, whether I knew them or not, "There but for the grace of God go I.")

Back to the question at hand: Should you scrap or should you not? More specifically, are you a person who should attempt to scrap when you are without much artistic talent, or would it be wiser to hire others to do your scrapping for you?

The course of true scrapbooking never did run smooth for some of us. Regardless of the fact my three sisters and I, on separate occasions, spent some serious prenatal time in the same womb, and disregarding the evidence we all squandered equal amounts of time in our youth learning the words to the theme songs from television shows such as *Gilligan's Island* and *Green Acres*, we are worlds apart when it comes to artistic talent. By which I mean to say some of us have a lot and some of us have a little.

Most people who stink artistically experienced one of two traumatic events in their youth: Either (1) they were raised in an underground hovel by people who ate cereal straight from the box and never allowed their children to experience natural sunlight until they went away to college, or (2) they were, like I was, put into a large empty cardboard box and made to keep quiet for hours on end. According to my mother (who to this day claims there was "no harm done!"), when I was two years old my family moved to a new house and, as evidenced in a photograph, placed me in an empty shipping container with some animal crackers. On that day of internment, remembered by some as "Moving Day," my mother was apparently experiencing morning sickness. That, plus the chaos of directing movers, painters, and various construction workers, led her to confine me, "for my own safety," to an empty appliance box. Being left to my own devices for such a lengthy period of time naturally left me traumatized and, it goes without saying, stunted in a creative sense.

Exactly what happened to thwart my youngest sister's creativity, on the other hand, is a question without an answer. This is a wild guess, but I suspect it has something to do with the fact she never was one to properly put away her crayons. She simply did not care about putting them back in the exact spot from whence they came, even though I specifically remember explaining to her more than once or twice, maybe a dozen times, that there is a right way and a wrong way to organize one's crayons. Yet always, always, she would just give me this look of hers that said, "Who cares? I don't care. I couldn't care less! What difference does it make? Shoo! Scat! Go away, you crazy thing, you!"

Imagine how hurtful and frustrating this was for *me*. Looking back I should have said, "Sticks and stones can break my bones but I can break your crayons," but instead I finally just threw my hands in the air and vowed never to color with her again, which is likely why she lacks artistic talent.

Anyway, whatever the reason, the fact is that she is also without much creative know-how. [Editor: Who cares? I don't care. It's a matter of sublime indifference.] *Que sera sera*, sister. Long story short, she and I have not had much success with scrapbooking on our own.

Moreover, we differ in our individual approaches to scrapbooking. She has always opted to try to pay our other, more talented sisters to create her scrapbooks for her—whereas I have paid dearly *not* to. It is mostly a matter of *admitting* to one's lack of artistic talent that puts one on a certain path in life, don't you think? Our fate, as Shakespeare himself once wrote, lies not within the stars (or within a cardboard box) but within ourselves. Could he have been inspired by the inkling that there would come a day when people would try to blame their lack of-scrapbooking talent on others? I'm not saying he did, I'm not saying he didn't—it's just a thought. Another thought is that we should accept full responsibility for our actions and stop blaming others for our personal struggles with creativity and claustrophobia. "Our remedies oft in ourselves do lie," either Shakespeare or my disorderly sister once said.

So, as we go forward we must understand that nearly everything in life happens for a reason. What is vital is for each of us to identify our strengths and make the most of them. Once we have made the most of our strengths, we can work on our weaknesses, or at the very least, enjoy a nice meal at one of the finer restaurants in town. And furthermore, "Be not afraid of greatness!" and while you're not being afraid of greatness, humbly remember, "The play *is* the thing!" So play! Have fun! And if you are cuckoo for scrapbooking, 'tis more the better. Anon, anon, and so on. [Editor's note: Who else thinks she wrote this chapter while eating cereal straight from a box?]

CHAPTER 17

'Tis the Scrapbooking Season

"Unseasonably" is one of my favorite words, so how delighted I am that this particular essay has everything to do with the way many of you avid scrapbookers work unseasonably. That is to say, you often can be found toiling away on pages featuring times of the year that are long gone. Times that came and then, just as quickly, went. Times that, sure, had a season, but are now nowhere in sight.

For example, it was April. There was the scent of spring wafting gently in the air, people were leaping about outdoors, uncovering their patio furniture while fighting the urge to sing out, "It's a beautiful day in the neighborhood!", planning their gardens, eyeing their golf clubs—you get the idea. So why, when I stopped by to visit my younger sister, did I find her bent over a table covered in red and green cardstock papers, candy-cane die-cuts, and a stack of holiday photos—with Ray Conniff's

"Here We Come A-Caroling" playing on the stereo? How weird, if not untimely, is that? It struck me as about as normal as playing John Philip Sousa on Christmas Eve.

Speaking of Sousa, have you ever noticed how he—one of the most patriotic songwriters to ever compose a note of jingoistic music—has a name that ends with the letters U-S-A? I *know*! It certainly makes you think about destiny. Interestingly enough, Sousa's well-loved "The Stars and Stripes Forever" is the song my father, week after week, year after year, blared from the intercom system in my childhood home on Saturday mornings to wake his children. To this day, whenever I hear Sousa I want to pull a pillow over my head and yell at my father to shut the hell up.

So [Editor: Amazing how some writers never worry about paragraph segue.], when I first walked in and found my sister sitting there in April—APRIL!—not only working on a Christmas scrapbook but in a Christmas atmosphere, I was *concerned*, so I asked in a concerned voice, "Sweetie, what the hell is going on here?"

She just laughed, patted my shoulder, and reminded me of my promise never to use swear words around her or her children.

Then she went on to explain how she genuinely enjoys making everything in the past perfect. She could hardly wait to create scrapbooks after big holiday events, so as not to lose the fresh recollections and subtle nuances surrounding the experience. At first I just chalked it up to postnatal dementia, but then she went on to explain that this is how she prefers to scrapbook. The only reason she was completing her Christmas scrapbooks in April rather than in January was due to the fact she had given birth in January—which had limited her scrapbooking time.

What I learned that day—which I am pleased to be passing along to you—is this important rule of creativity: Scrapbooking time has no season!

So, if you are eager to work on Easter die-cuts in October? *Get cracking!* Want to treat yourself to a Halloween crop in April? *Nobody's going to say boo.* Feel like creating a St. Patrick's Day page in August? *Good luck!* And if it's Christmas Eve and you feel like scrapbooking your Fourth of July photos? *Enjoy yourself!* And while you're at it, put on some marching music.

CHAPTER 18

Excuses, Excuses

When my first child was born his grandmother provided a beautiful baby book in which to record important dates and keep his first-year photos and mementos. And I did.

Two years later, when my second child was born, his grandmother gave us another adorable baby scrapbook in which to record his first year.

And I will. Just as soon as I get a minute.

Thank you for not throwing this book across the room, unless you did; and if you did, I can't say that I blame you. Occasionally, my inability to get my scrap together makes me ill. Sometimes I feel as if I don't deserve to have children. But then I remind myself that I never missed a day when it came to administering my babies' vitamins or fluoride drops; I almost never failed to pick them up when they were hurt or when they were waiting in front of their school in the rain, ruined art proj-

ect in hand; I rarely if ever forget to attend parent/teacher con-
ferences. Furthermore, neither of my sons has ever had head
lice or scurvy or a bad case of rickets; they sleep on clean sheets;
they hardly ever go to bed hungry; they have been to Disneyland
twice. So it's not as if I am a terrible parent.

It is also not like I am my younger sister, who is a wonderful
parent. A professional scrapbooker, she had her first child's
beautiful pink leather prebirth album completed before the
child's umbilical cord was cut. Speaking of which, a remnant of
that cord can be found on page five of this baby's second album,
an album that was completed before my sister's breast milk
came in. Volume three, a matching album in a set of who knows
how many, commenced by celebrating the baby's first smile,
which occurred on the same day mother and child returned
home from the hospital.

I honestly do not know how you scrapping new mothers do
it. But then, I have no idea of how professional basketball play-
ers make those three-pointers. Even if you took away the crowd
and the opposing team, I could stand there alone on the court
for hours and hours, shooting and shooting, throwing and
throwing the ball until my arms where dislocated, and never
come close to making a basket.

But enough about basketball. Let's look at why babies are
the most photographed subjects in the world. For obvious reasons, parents cannot resist taking a picture every time there is a
new milestone—so at *least* twice a day for the first year.

After my child was born, when he was nearing the age of pu-
berty, I came across an article about creating a memory book of
a baby's first year that was so filled with useful information I just
had to cut it out. It outlined everything from how to record a

child's daily growth to ways in which a child's "firsts" can be documented. It was a complete three-page guide to creating a scrapbook that will give your child a foundation for a lifetime of self-esteem.

My favorite line from the article was a cautionary one: "Give yourself permission not to scrapbook every photograph of your baby. In fact, now and then give yourself permission to forget you even have a baby! Go ahead, take a shower; your husband can handle the camera while you're shampooing your hair!" Now that is advice worth remembering.

Where were we? Guilt disorients me. So listen, take some advice from that article I cut out and have since misplaced. Take the time to create a scrapbook that your child will cherish when he or she is older. I know you will since you understand the consequences if you do not. If you don't understand what I mean by "consequences," you had better understand what "lightning rod" means because that's what you will be for your children whenever they are struck with a need to blame someone for their unhappiness.

CHAPTER 19

Cherish the Thoughts

My childhood was lousy. Not that I was ever denied food or water (unless you count the times I was left to spend the night with Grandma B., who couldn't be torn away from *The Lawrence Welk Show* even if you shouted "I'm thirsty!" or "Fire!"—not that I tried that more than once), but never, not on a single one of my family's yearly trips to Disneyland, was I allowed to pose with a Dopey Dwarf or have my picture taken with Snow White. Which, if you'll excuse me for saying so, really bites. Not once did it occur to my mother, keeper of the camera, to take a picture of her children standing next to a lovable character with big ears like Mickey Mouse or Grandpa, either of whom would have gladly mimed "Cheese!" While I could go on about missed photo opportunities at the world's happiest places, I won't. You can clearly see where I'm going with this: There were opportunities; they were lost.

(By the way, in *no way* is this one of those "I'm a shameless loser thanks to mother dearest" stories. Of course not! I love, admire, and appreciate my mother and she has the WORLD'S GREATEST MOM ceramic mug to prove it. She is somebody who gave it her all long before the advent of cordless phones or flat, sensible shoes. Mom worked wonders with what she had. It was no fault of her own that all she had with which to photograph her children was a Polaroid camera that resembled a small accordion and was a bitch to set up. [Editor: Writers with lazy minds resort to profanity.])

That hurt. But not as much as the deprivation I feel when comparing the shreds of my youthful memories to the vibrant, vivid, tangible memories belonging to persons I know who are currently children. But never mind.

I adore these auspicious children (some of them call me Aunt) smiling up from their personal scrapbook pages. They are lucky to have adoring scrapbooking mothers who could write the book on raising happy kids, and I sincerely hope they do.

To be honest, these privileged youngsters are not the only children who make me a little agitated. No, not a day goes by that I don't fret about the world's *other* children (some of them call me Mom) who go to bed hungry for attention. My quest to document their lives, I am almost ashamed to say, has amounted to one failed effort after another.

The trouble is I am always terribly busy. And when I'm not busy, I'm terribly lazy. The real problem is that when I find myself with time or energy to spare, I'm overwhelmed by responsibility or the desire to do, *oh*, nothing. Furthermore, successfully creating scrapbooks that do justice to the love and admiration I have for my two sons—well, this seems beyond my current capabilities. What I'm trying to say here is . . . [Editor: Let's just say you're lazy, honesty being the best policy, and leave it at that.] Sounds good to me.

All, however, is not beyond hope, for I have major plans. The more I learn about scrapbooking, the more I realize the importance of creating legacy-type scrapbooks for my kids, someday.

Someday, when I have a few thousand fancy-free dollars to spend on scrapbook supplies, I will take that cash and rush right out to purchase every single thing necessary to create aesthetically as well as asthmatically pleasing scrapbooks for my sons, both of whom have come to the misguided conclusion that something vital is missing from their childhood—like visual documentation. Unfortunately, they have never accepted as truth my flimsy reminders that it is the thoughts that count. "Cherish the thoughts," I tell them. "Cherish your memories, they belong to you and they always will, nobody can take them away," I say.

Still, they want scrapbooks. They have seen their cousins' scrapbooks. They know I have large storage boxes of photographs under my bed. They know I am writing a book about scrapbooking. All of which is why, cross my heart and hope to die-cut, I will create scrapbooks for them, someday.

Someday, when I have a few months to catalog the contents of those boxes under my bed that contain in excess of something like two thousand loose and unmarked pictures—half of which were taken on a trip to Washington during the most miserable peak of humidity ever recorded, which is why we all look like flood victims just pulled from the Potomac and photographed to show what dripping-wet dead people look like. Anyway, here's the thing: Someday I will organize those pictures.

Someday, when I'm old and gray, when the children are far away and I'm thinking of them and the way they never return my calls, then, that day, maybe I will finally have the time, money, and focus to get scrappin'. Meanwhile, I hope (so far in vain) to stop comparing my life and the lives of my children to the lives of our more photographed family and friends, because it only makes me feel lousy.

CHAPTER 20

How to Start a Scrapbooking Business

If you have a sincere interest in starting your own scrapbook business, you are, with all due respect, a fool. No, seriously, you sort of are. That said, however, if you have a sincere interest in starting a potentially lucrative scrapbook business, you have come to the right place. A place I call Hell, but hey! That's just me and this is about helping *you*. And help you I will, because I just spent an entire year running my scrapbook business into the ground! It is remarkable, really, what a marvelous teacher failure is. Oh, the lessons I learned! The places I went! [Editor: Into debt, for starters.] Yes, that humiliating and somewhat debilitating experience cleaned out my savings account and temporarily wiped the smile off my face. Yes, the truth is I lost everything. [Editor: Not true, she gained a good ten pounds.]

Believe you me, I could write a book about failure—but

that's not the point. The point is to write only a chapter. A chapter that will, let us keep our fingers crossed, prevent you from making the same dreadful, demeaning, and costly mistakes.

Oh, relax. This is not as bad as it sounds, as long as you keep a positive attitude and all of your receipts and do just as I say, not as I did. What is important here is how much I know now that I did not know then, all of which I am more than delighted to share with you, free of charge. Minus, of course, the price [Editor: She hopes it was full price.] you paid for this book. A book that, by the way, makes a lovely gift.

Okay, back to beeswax. If you are pretty certain you have a real talent for creating something—anything at all, big or small, cute or clever, matte or glossy—anything that is photo-safe and acid-free, which scrapbookers need or at least want, you may as well quit your boring day job and start minding your own little business. Or, as I like to say, minding your own damn business.

Now, the first thing you will want to do when starting your scrapbooking business is to be a guest on Oprah's show. Of course, you will never be on *Oprah*, not in a million years, yet you will certainly *want* to be. I know I wanted to be and would have been if prayers and a certain series of phone calls had not gone unanswered. So if it's any consolation whatsoever to you, I never once made it on *Oprah* and—bless your heart—neither will you.

In the real world, my friend, you will find strangers who call you "my friend" and you will find it necessary to make a big to-do every time you turn around if you hope to sell whatever it is you have there. This is not as exciting as it sounds. My suggestion—and keep in mind that it's just a suggestion—is to start by asking scrapbook retailers to pay good money for your unique product. Now, even if you call them "my friend," and even if they are related to you, the likelihood of convincing a substantial group of people to order your product is not so good either. In fact, you have a better chance of being invited to Oprah's house for Christmas dinner. Still, fate is funny (whereas failure is not), and you may against all odds end up doing just fine.

After all, scrapbookers collectively spent something in the neighborhood of like, what, forty billion dollars last year on photo-friendly supplies? So all you must do, really, is step up to the plate and demand your piece of the pie. This is not as simple as it sounds, so just try to avoid the humble pie by working harder and smarter than everybody else.

And remember, remember, remember: Timing is everything. Just so you know, the best time to start a scrapbook business in your basement was about ten years ago. There was enormous opportunity back then. Now, however, you really must burn the midnight oil, keep a stiff upper lip, and be a blood relation to someone who is already well established in the scrapbooking industry.

I'm just repeating what I heard, but the worst mistake you can make is to disregard the fact that scrapbooking is no longer a cottage industry. Today, scrapbooking is big business and big businesses have a wee bit more know-how, clout, and creativity than any anonymous upstart with an impetuous idea.

Today, it is risky to sink your life savings into a small-scale business venture believing that the sky is the limit. Just because you minored in art and enjoy scrapbooking is no reason to get your kids' hopes up by waving your graphic designs in their faces and shouting, "We are going to be so rich!" I mean, give me a break.

Next to a unique product, an appearance on *Oprah*, good

timing, and family connections, you need loyal employees. This is why you must build company solidarity by sending out for pizza, giving them paychecks, and having office picnics, holiday parties, and even employee-of-the-month morale boosters. Call us outlandish, but my office crowd took the whole thing a step further and organized a cookie-baking and hair-coloring party. The four of us spent an entire evening and all of our petty cash changing our various natural hair colors to a dark, shiny mahogany, which turned us all into stunning redheads. All except for one gal, who had previously used an inferior product called Party Girl Blonde. When the henna mixture was applied to her head it turned her hair a slightly greenish color, which greatly upset her since at the time she was seriously hoping to get a callback from the folks at *Who Wants to Marry a Multimillionaire*.

Speaking of which, if you want to be a millionaire you must, from the get-go, stay on top of all matters financial. This is not as simple as it sounds and, quite frankly, I failed to listen enough to either my accountant or my business partner, who would slap herself on the forehead when she heard me saying things like "Hey! It's only money!" or "Margin call? What the heck is a margin call?" or "Don't be an idiot—we'll make more money than Oprah if we do it my way!"

No, none of that funny business for you. Seriously, it is best not to talk any more about this chapter of my life. Let's just call it Chapter Eleven, and leave it at that.

People have asked me to my face, "How does it feel to have your business fail?" And I, being wiser for the experience, more contemplative, more eager to do whatever I can to prevent the suffering of others, will tell these curious people the truth: "It feels really bad."

Photos Are Forever

Remember when you were a child, how satisfying it was to say something snotty like, "Take a picture, it lasts longer!" when some-one was seemingly, and most likely unknowingly, staring at you?

Well, pictures taken today do last years—light years longer than pictures snapped back then. This is all thanks to the genius, whoever she was, who created modern archival photo-page pro-tectors and other nuke-proof, molecularly advanced develop-ments in safeguarding photos and scrapbooking supplies.

Thanks to this new technology, modern film is not so flimsy, modern paper and ink are safe enough to eat and drink, and modern scrapbooking glues are lean and clean. Any item that is not already photo-safe can be treated with a nonflammable spray so as to preserve it long after the people in the photo-graph are of interest to anyone.

Let me tell you something exciting: So advanced are present-day archival techniques that there's an excellent chance many of the scrapbooks created this year could, one day, hundreds of years from now, end up on another planet far, far away. It is entirely within the realm of possibility that an eon from now a creature in another galaxy will show her friends a scrapbook she bought on Cosmic eBay. As she gleefully explains that the beings in the photographs are primitive people known as Earthlings, they will all have a good laugh at our expense. "Look at the antennae on these Earthlings—two fingers behind each others' heads!" [laughter] "Oh, my! What small buttocks they all have!" [belly laughs] "And only *two* eyes!" [they giggle their pointed little heads off].

Currently, my primary concern leans more toward preserving photographs for the next generation of Earthlings. Which is why, for the sake of those of you who are new to scrapbooking, we will now review photo preservation techniques and materials. The essential ones, anyway—or at the very least, the ones I can think of without doing any research.

So as not to be too wishy-washy or mind-numbingly scientific, I ask you first to consider acid and lignin. Notice, if you have not already noticed, that bona fide scrapbooking supplies contain no acid or lignin because these elements are to your photos what sunbeams are to your unprotected skin: damaging, aka damn-aging. What's more, according to the scrapbook intelligentsia, all of whom had the wherewithal to conduct extensive, and one would hope, government-approved research, lignin will turn your favorite photos and patterned papers into pulp in a matter of centuries, if not decades. Same goes for acid. So, to be clear, neither lignin nor acid nor words such as asinine belong in your scrapbooks.

Now, you don't have to be a rocket scientist to know that photographs are best kept in protective, acid-free slipcovers and fireproof storage boxes. Also, photographs do not belong anywhere near children who are dripping ice cream cones, Popsicles, or the melted butter from corn on the cob. Also children with drippy noses must be kept away from scrapbooks until they have recovered from their colds. Attention and thanks should be paid to the wise mother, the one I recently heard about or possibly dreamt about, who keeps her works of art in a specially made, salad bar–type kiosk with a sneeze-protector shield so her children can safely enjoy their individual scrapbooks regardless of their state of health.

Many of you surely have thoughtful inquiries regarding what is safe to include in a scrapbook. To answer all of your questions, however, I would have to conduct an in-depth research project of my own, which is simply out of the question. Lately I can't find the time to complete a scrapbook page or get a mammogram, busy as I am making up stuff to write in this book. So I suggest you conduct your own experimentation using my patent-free Microwave-Type Method of Testing, which, if not conducted properly, may singe those dark hairs growing above your upper lip. (If you just said, "But I don't have any dark hairs growing above my upper lip," you have obviously never looked into one of those super-magnifying mirrors.)

In order to perform the Microwave-Type Method of Testing, it is necessary to (1) place the decorative item in the middle of your scrapbook, (2) stand clear, (3) wait and see if the decorative item starts to crackle or shoot sparks, and, if it does, (4) remove the item promptly, before damage occurs. If, however, nothing happens, good. Even then, keep in mind, the item

CHAPTER 22

Surefire Photo Safety

When I was a child my family's house nearly burned to the ground. You'll have to take my word for it since there are no photographs of the incinerating incident and the only scars are emotional.

It still burns me that nobody took pictures. "Apparently," a parent said, "everybody was too busy dragging furniture and rugs and children out of the house to stop and think about taking photos."

Sadder still, at least half of the family's photographs went up in smoke. Nothing but ashes. Gone, negatives and all. Thankfully, the remaining photos were safe, as always, within the plastic slip covers of my mother's wallet.

Today, of course, most families have photos to burn, so to speak. By which I mean more photos than they know what to do with. The best of them, naturally, are bound in beautiful and elaborate memory books—which is why any person worth her weight in gold glitter needs a photo-protection plan covering every likely scenario, including the one where the cat spontaneously combusts. If you don't have a plan, you're playing with fire, my friend.

This is not meant to alarm you. No, there's no reason to make you fret the way the United States Department of Forest Services with their anxiety-inducing tactics made me fret as a child. Their message, via Smokey the Bear, was a burden: "Only *you* can prevent forest fires!" Only I? Why point the finger at me, a little matchless girl who rarely saw the forest for the trees? How about: "Only careless campers, chain-smokers, and pyromaniacs can prevent forest fires, unless there's an electrical storm and then, thank God, nobody's to blame for the act"?

Not knowing [Editor: Or caring] where I was going with that, let us consider instead today's hot topic: How to keep your photos safe when your house burns to the ground. It is simpler than it sounds if you follow these commonsense guidelines and precautions:

1. The mother of all fire-safety rules: Insist your children live somewhere other than at home. Why? Can you guess how many fires were started by youngsters last year? Maybe two hundred or so, you say? Try 100,000. Yes, that's right—100,000 fires were started by kids last year alone! Sparky the Fire Dog will back me up on this.

2. If you suddenly wake up and smell smoke, shout "Fire!" unless you are in a theater and it's crowded

and there really is no fire. Next, evacuate! Grab
your scrapbooks and small pets and run like crazy
for the nearest exit. You won't have to worry about
your children since they are not in the house. [See
Rule #1.]

3. Protect your photos from water damage. Trust me,
   you don't want to save your photos from the flames
   only to have them liquidated by water, water that is
   sure to be fast-moving, hard-hitting, and flying in all
   directions. It will do no good whatsoever to shriek
   or repeatedly demand the firefighters keep the
   water away from your scrapbooks. In fact, if you
   repeatedly bother the firefighters you may find the
   water from their hoses vigorously pushing you and
   your scrapbooks into the neighbors' front yard.

4. Do not ever, as long as you live, go running back
   into your burning house to save a scrapbook.
   Instead, ask one of your neighbors to do it. Of
   course, the neighbor will see you are only joking yet
   also a little hysterical, which would be a good time
   to request a camera and some vellum, I mean
   Valium.

5. For safekeeping, a fireproof safe for your photo-safe
   scrapbooks is a safe bet. As a backup, however,
   keep your photos' negatives at somebody else's
   house. (Not mine, since I'm not a negative person.)

6. As a final precaution, make copies of all your
   pictures and pages. Using a digital camera,

photograph your entire scrapbook collection, then
e-mail copies to your family and friends and ask
them to use the memory on their computers to save
your memories.

So those are the rules. Fire safety rules, unfortunately, only
go so far. Even though you are now equipped to prevent yourself
and your scrapbooks from getting burned, you should abandon
hope of saving anything else. This is a good reason to consider
increasing your homeowners insurance policy to cover the loss
of or damage to your scrap supplies; which, for the typical
scrapbooker, are worth somewhere in the neighborhood of, oh,
what? Eight, nine hundred thousand dollars? Your call, but trust
me, you'll sleep better at night knowing you will be able to re-
place your supplies—at least your basic supplies—if disaster
strikes.

CHAPTER 23

National Scrapbook Contest Winner!

Like you, I would not mind winning a national contest. In fact, I have always wanted to be a winner. Not an Oscar-winning winner, but a national winner nonetheless, a champion of some sort in a national contest. Not just *any* national contest, but specifically a contest that celebrates the best scrapbook page layouts in the country. By country, I mean the United States of America, since this is after all my country, land that I love.

Down the road, once I have more experience under my belt (a "genuine leather" reversible one, by the way, which was recently purchased at a 50 percent discount thanks to an in-store coupon), I may have the confidence to conjure up an even bigger dream of winning a worldwide contest. As it is, currently, and given what I know about the never-ending scrapbooking going on in Canada, Great Britain, and Japan, I don't believe deep down in my heart that I could seriously capture more than an honorable mention in a scrapbooking competition between the best and most left-brained from around the globe. But who knows? Stranger things have happened. I mean, look at the people who end up winning the lottery. Long shots all.

Anyway, it would be a goal well-met if I could win a national scrapbooking contest. I personally know people who have done it in the past, and that always helps. One of them is related to me, which makes me believe if she can achieve it perhaps I could too. All I'd have to do is start scrapbooking every day like she does; teach crop workshops like the ones she is always teaching; and host frequent scrapbooking parties like she hosts.

Better yet, I might simply ask her to design a layout for me to submit in the contest. Then I'd be a shoo-in!

Scrapbooking competitions, from what little I know, are extremely friendly. They are the sort of contests set up solely and ultimately to encourage creative page ideas. You'll find no booing or hissing here. Nor will you find judges who ended up being slapped with fines because they are found guilty of having taken bribes. And while I know some wise guy once said "Never say never," I nonetheless think it is safe to say you will *never* read in the news an account of how one top scrapbooker purposely whacked another top scrapbooker on the knee—or worse, on the hand!—with the illegal and malicious intention of putting her competition out of the running. No, none of those dirty tricks in this industry, which is a relief.

That said, there are prizes and plenty of prestige for the winner. Nobody's going to make a movie about you, but still, it is easy to imagine nods of silent approval all around whenever you walk into a crop party.

If I were to win a scrapbooking contest—and that's a pretty big "if" [Editor: So big, in fact, that it rhymes with OUT OF THE QUESTION.]—the first thing I'd do would be to pinch myself with a sharp pair of grippers to make sure I wasn't dreaming. Once proven awake, I would take great delight in knowing that my scrapbooking sisters and friends would have to look at me in a new light: a glowing, soft-focus limelight. A light that would prove them all wrong, revealing me to be an excellent scrapbooker after all. It might make a few of them so bitter they would not talk to me for weeks, but that would be a small price to pay for national glory and attention.

Here is my dream. I am sitting at home, reading to my children from, oh, say, the Bible, or some etiquette book written by Judith Martin, when the telephone rings. My youngest son answers the phone politely, rather than loudly or rudely, and I hear him say, "Yes, ma'am, my mother is currently at home. Kindly wait just a moment."

Then, rather than yelling "MOM! PHONE!" before rushing outside or upstairs, he will take the time to walk into the room where I am sitting and hand me the receiver.

"Hello," I will say in that confident way some people have. (One thing is certain, I will not say, "Hello?" in that unsure way that sounds more like a question, more like a question that asks, "Are you still there? Do you still want to talk with me?")

Then I will hear a voice on the other end of the line saying, "Congratulations! It is my pleasure to announce that you have just been chosen as one of the best scrapbookers in the nation!"

"I? Really?" I will respond humbly.

"Yes, of course, you! Really!" The caller will laugh lightly.

"Get out!" I will respond coyly.

"No, I am quite serious; you are among the top ten scrapbookers in the country according to—"

"Shut up!" I will respond excitedly.

"—our panel of ju . . . what did you just say?" she will ask abruptly.

"I said, 'Shut up,' but all I meant was 'Get out,' by which I mean to say, 'Are you pulling my leg?' " I will explain.

"Ah. Well, no, I am not pulling your leg, you are indeed one of this week's national winners," she will assure me.

"WOW! So then I won! You like me, you really like me!" I will practically scream.

"Well, we liked your page layout. . . ." the contest official will clarify.

"Get out!" I will answer.

"Well, really . . . again, congratulations!" she will say.

"Shut up!" I will say, thrilled.

"Bye-bye, now!" she will quickly add before hanging up.

"Is this a joke? Is this Stan? Stan? Stan, you dog! Ha! You crazy son of a—"

[*Click!*]

"Stan? Stan?"

[*Loud repetitive phone beeping.*]

"Ha ha!" I will laugh as it hits me that it was not Stan, because I don't even know anybody named Stan. I once knew a guy named *Stew*, but he is now in the witness protection plan or with Save the Whales, I can never remember which.

So then, realizing the call was genuine, I will hop around the room, stopping only long enough to yell to my kids, "I won! Your mother is a national scrapbook winner!"

Suddenly, I will rush right up to the mirror and start performing the song I usually save for the shower, "Hey now! I'm a rock star, nah, nah, nah, naaaaah!"

And I will continue singing until either I collapse from exhilaration and exhaustion or one of my kids calls the cops.

Anyway, it could happen; I could win.

CHAPTER 24

Tragedy Plus Time Equals Humor?

My sides ache. Last night I went to my sister's house to make a scrapbook for our mother and, oh, did I laugh until my cheeks were a blur of tears. So you might say I laughed until I cried.

But you would be wrong. What I cried is "Uncle . . . ?" Or more specifically, "Uncle Bill?" I was crying out an answer to my sister, who was holding up an old photo of a kid with a struck-by-lightning hairdo, grinning manically while lifting up his shirt and pointing at his grotesquely protruding rib cage.

"Who do you think this is?" my sister mischievously asked.

"Uh . . . Uncle Bill?" I guessed.

"Uncle Bill? Did you say *Uncle Bill*? No-*ho*-hoo!" my sister gleefully replied as she flipped the photo over to reveal the name that had been, many, many years ago, when I was nine or seven or possibly six years old, written in our mother's handwriting. "It is . . . ," she wheezed with laughter, ". . . YOU!" Then I watched as she doubled over and, weak with giggles, rolled out of her chair and onto the floor.

"Well, I'll be darned," I said reaching for that amusing little photograph that was begging to be destroyed inasmuch as it misrepresented me as a gap-toothed girl lacking shame, hair-grooming implements, and breasts. There was no date on the photo, but my sister swore it had to be the summer before I went away to college.

As any seasoned scrapbooker will tell you, it is necessary to use acid-free paper to keep photos from degrading over time. What nobody tells you, however, is that the preserved photos may degrade *you* later in life. Here's the thing about old photos: Some of them are simply not worth saving. Too ugly for words, too ugly even for use as coasters, these embarrassing photos need not be preserved.

Right off the top of my head I can think of a dozen reasons why photographs portraying people, namely myself, with unflattering hairdos and unsightly orthodontia are worth a thousand worries. Without carefully checking historical facts, I feel confident reporting that while every era had its hideous hairstyles, the 1970s were the worst. During those years—because we did not know any better and all of our friends were doing it—my sisters and I, time and time again, posed for photographs sporting damaged permanent waves (the worn fuzzy look), sloppy shags (to match the carpet in our bedrooms), and pointless bangs (our clowning glory, as it were). And my brothers' hair was never much better, thanks to a genetic disposition toward gravity-defying cowlicks.

It's weird. Our generation was the first in human history to have access to both shampoo and conditioner plus conveniently located, supposedly "trained" hairstylists. And yet we always looked worse than our ancestors—the ones who lived in trees and were dragged around by their hair.

Of course, you don't care about my hair or photo problems. You have enough problems of your own to worry about. Chances are either you or someone in your family is an unreasonable photo-protector who gathers old pictures to her bosom as if each one were a long-lost child in need of saving.

True scrapaholics are instantly recognizable by their inability to throw away a photograph. My older sister is no exception. Talk about digging up old memories—her scrapbooking table is always piled high with photos. She has literally hundreds, and I do mean hundreds, of long-forgotten family photos that she somehow inherited and has cared for over the years.

To the outsider it may look as if she is hanging on to these photos for the fun of it, but, no, that's not it. This sister of mine simply believes that, as there are relatively few of them, each old family photo is worth saving. She refuses to allow any snapshot to be torn apart, cut in half, mustachioed in black ink, or damaged in any similar fashion. In her mind, old photos are heirlooms no matter how loony-looking the rightful heir.

My sister also feels each photo has a story to tell; or at least each photo prompts tales that can be told. These photo stories have always made me laugh and laugh—that is, until the aforementioned photo showed up. You know how it is when you're laughing at a photo of your elderly uncle, and then suddenly you see it is actually a picture of yourself from long ago, and that brings up all sorts of bothersome issues? And then to top it off, when you demand that the photo be destroyed, your older sibling—as the oldest sibling often will do—behaves as if she is the boss of you, refusing your plea? Well, let me tell you, the party's over when that happens.

The unattractive person featured in the photo, you would think, should decide the fate of the photo, but not in my family. It matters not how humiliating a snapshot may be, my sister still treats it as an honest-to-goodness treasure. That's because she is crazy—at least and especially about photographic imagery.

Still, how embarrassing for this photo-keeping sister to be chased around her dining room table while holding a photo high in the air as I tried to grab it away from her. "It's part of our family's history!" she squealed. "Its details are part of our family's legacy! It belongs to our prodigy, not to you!" I told her the word she was looking for was "progeny," and that she was being ridiculously rude and unreasonable, but still she refused to hand over that offensive picture that portrayed me as a young Uncle Bill.

Not surprisingly, it wasn't long before I said my farewells. Gathering my pride, my sides sore from laughing, I announced that I felt a bout of shingles coming on and had to leave. While walking toward my car, however, I was chuckling to myself over the memories of those old family photographs. Especially the snapshot of "Uncle Bill"—which was now, unbeknownst to my sister, tucked inside my coat pocket. (Ha!)

CHAPTER 25

A Mother's Scrapbook

Months before my mother's seventy-fifth birthday my sister started planning the big party and, even bigger, The Scrapbook. In her mind, any noteworthy occasion is nothing unless it comes complete with a large, elaborate scrapbook documenting past highlights leading up to the current occasion. An occasion at which, you can bet, she and a few of the other females in my family will take plenty more photos for reference at future significant occasions, which will be complete only if a large scrapbook is created.

This particular scrapbook, celebrating my mother's past three-quarters of a century, was intended to highlight her life. Per my sister's explicit instructions, each sibling was to create one (1) family page. In addition, we were to also design pages featuring each of our children with their grandmother. Moreover, we were to provide thoughtful personal letters to our mother touting her most outstanding characteristics and accomplishments. Also, we were to . . . blah, blah, blah.

You get the idea; it was going to be a very nice book, really, but, hello! I have *two* children and was given only two months' notice. If you've learned nothing else from this book so far, you should know that for me, this task was daunting.

Immediately my sister Judy started calling with reminders that my pages were due. For lack of a caller ID, I usually answered the phone. At first her calls were pleasant. She would even invite me to her house to scrapbook. Here is a sample from one of our many conversations:

ME: Hello.

JUDY: Hi! Hey, how are those scrapbook pages coming?

ME: Fine.

JUDY: *Really*?

ME: Really. Could not be better.

JUDY: Do you need any help?

ME: No.

JUDY: Are you sure?

ME: Yes.

JUDY: When can I see them?

ME: When do you need them?

JUDY: As I told you yesterday, I need them *today*, if we're going to make this the scrapbook Mom deserves. I mean, she's our *mother*, she gave us *life*. The least we can do is give her a beautiful scrapbook commemorating *her* life, right?

ME: Right, and thanks for once again not dramatically overstating everything, but if you had asked me I

would have suggested we give our mother postage
stamps for her birthday. She needs stamps more
than she needs a scrapbook.

JUDY: [silence]

ME: Really, every time I call her she's either paying her
bills or just heading out the door to the post office
to buy stamps.

JUDY: Just finish your pages, okay?

ME: Fine, no sweat. Good-bye.

JUDY: Good-bye!

Then, when there were only two weeks to go, this same sister called and told me everyone else had completed their pages and the book was really turning out to be wonderful, better than she dreamed—all she needed from me were my three or four pages.

The night before my mother's birthday my sister called again.

ME: Hello?

JUDY: Tonight. I need your pages *tonight*.

ME: You need them tonight?

JUDY: Yes.

ME: *Tonight*?! *Uh-oh.* . . .

JUDY: What?

ME: Then I am going to need some serious help.

JUDY: [unprintable response]

ME: Hope you don't kiss your children with that mouth.

JUDY: This is ridiculous! You're the only one in the
family who has failed to complete your layouts!

Because of you the scrapbook won't be finished.

Because of you Mom's birthday will be spoiled.

Because of you the family collectively, once again,

fails to reach its potential. You *always* do this!

ME: Not true. You are just trying to make me feel

terrible.

JUDY: You should feel terrible. Stay up all night, what-

ever it takes, but do not come to the party unless you

have your completed pages.

ME: Fine. Good-bye.

JUDY: Good-bye.

The next night my mother cried tears of joy when she opened her present and found a scrapbook created for her by her family. The scrapbook, a beautifully organized visual compilation of her life so far, was extraordinary. My sister was right—much better than postage stamps. Everyone made a huge fuss over the book and the party was a great success.

The best moment came at the end of the evening. People were putting tables away, the vacuum was running, dishes were clinking, tired babies were crying, and I was doing my best to grab my kids and make the usual early exit, but something stopped me, something made me reconsider and stay awhile. It was my youngest sister's request that I just once actually stay and help with the cleanup. She had a point (or, rather, the large butcher knife she was holding had a point) so I graciously offered to pitch in. As I walked back toward the kitchen, there sat the sister who had done most of the pre-party planning and the bulk of the work on the scrapbook. There she sat in a big armchair, in a state of bliss; completely unaware of the chaos surrounding her as she turned the pages of the scrapbook she had put together for our mother.

Party food: $300.

Party decorations: $150.

Scrapbook supplies: $2,000 plus change.

The look on my sister's face when I told her my pages were finished in time for the party: Stunned. (And, yes, priceless.)

CHAPTER 26

Animal Slacker

Ask anyone and she'll tell you a smart reason to create scrapbooks for your children is to establish plenty of verifiable proof that they had an upstanding upbringing. For this same reason, no wise scrapbooker—unless she suffers from allergies, germ phobias, or a keen sense of smell—would deny her young the rewarding opportunity to care for a cute, face-licking family pet that can be prominently featured in family photo albums.

If you fail to do either of the above, years from now your grown children will whine accusatorially about how you never gave them an animal to call their own. The only childhood recollection likely to result in more complaint would be the way you once interrupted your son's soccer game by running onto the playing field crying, "My baby! My *poor baby!*" when he landed head first after tripping on his untied shoelace.

Accidentally embarrassing or disappointing your children

like this will, trust me, play havoc with your happiness down the road, and is nearly as damaging as forgetting to take family vacations or overlooking your children's birthdays from time to time.

For the record, vacations and birthdays are a piece of cake compared to animal ownership. Still, difficult or not, you have little choice in the matter: Either you get your children a pet and take plenty of photographs or suffer the consequences.

When my oldest child starting asking for a dog I was forced to ask myself the hard questions: Do we have a fenced yard? No, we do not. Am I a dog person? Not really. Am I at least ready to accept the daunting responsibilities of dog ownership? Not even.

So I went straight out and got my son a puppy *puppet*. This lifelike creature could have passed for the real thing in a photograph but, alas, did not fool my child for a minute. He tugged the dancing puppet off my arm before I got through the first verse of "Oh Where, Oh Where, Has My Little Dog Gone." Later that day he showed me his new pet, a moth. The little creature lay in the palm of his hand, twitching like it had flown too close to one too many flames. "Its name is Spot," said the pet's new owner. (We were in the middle of reading and rereading and rereading the *Spot the Dog* series.) With a look of joy mixed with fear on his young face, my son added that this moth did not want to be "swatted back to heaven" like the other moths I happened upon in our house. I was stunned at how low and mean I must look in the eyes of my child. [Editor: Not to mention the eyes of God.] I had to do something redemptive, something unselfish.

The next day we had our first of many pets, a cat.

I decided not to worry that I myself am not a cat person or even a tolerant person. This wasn't, after all, about me. This was about helping my child like me again. It was about teaching my son to be a caring and loving person who would not grow up to blame his mother for every little unhappiness in his life. A cat, I told myself, will teach a slew of valuable lessons and be a best friend at the same time, a best friend who provides loyalty and affection.

Loyalty, affection, and photographic evidence of what an excellent parent I am. This pet thing is gold! *Gold* I tell you! Or so I told myself.

Who was I trying to kid? The truth is pets do not always work out for the best—especially if it turns out you have an uncanny knack for picking nonphotogenic pets with bizarre behavioral problems. [Editor: Birds of a feather. . . .] Also, the pets I picked in the past—a dog, cat, a hamster, a couple turtles—like fish and houseguests always smelled bad after three days. Furthermore and unfortunately, most of our animals' odors, though nothing to sniff at, were a breath of fresh air compared to their remarkably destructive temperaments, claws, and teeth. Especially our first cat, Bailey.

Usually cats, especially kittens, are as cute as a button or a baby in photographs. A large tabby, our Bailey was anything but. Despite her beautiful orange-striped fur, Bailey was as gray and dismal as they come. She came to us from a seemingly nice family. In retrospect, however, those folks were far too nervous, eager, and gleeful as they crated the cat, handed her over, and waved away my offers to pay them something.

Once we got our new pet home she promptly threw a hissy fit, demonstrating out-of-the-box urination, outrageous aggression, random destructiveness, and wanton disobedience. She repeatedly ignored my patient attempts to teach her proper pet etiquette starting with the first rule of housecats: No scratching humans.

Finally, I called a cat expert for advice. She said to cat-proof our house and create an atmosphere that would alleviate our kitty's separation anxiety. "Think like a cat," she also advised. "Get down on her level, imitate her movements, until you understand what motivates her," was her final harebrained suggestion.

"Well, thank you," I said, "for nothing."

Instead I just did what seemed natural. When the cat misbehaved I would firmly shout, "Sit!" or "No!" or "I wish you had fewer than nine lives!" before tossing her squeaky toys out into the street.

Anyway, Bailey did not work out well for us—but that's another story. The point is, you must give pet ownership a shot. It works out surprisingly well for most people. In fact, many people would never consider life without a pet. These people tell me their fondest memories include their dogs and cats. Most of them have beautiful scrapbook pages to back these claims up. I admire you animal people—you who are a dog's best friend, the cat's meow, the good and loving canary caregivers—but you are not my breed of people.

Don't get me wrong; I'd never harm a flea-bitten animal; I don't even eat meat or wear fur. I do, however, wear wool—and, for that reason, if I see an egg-laying moth in my house, I will swat it back to heaven in no time flat.

CHAPTER 27

Circa 1968

If memory serves, my oldest sister, the one who grew up to own her own scrapbook store, created her first scrapbook more than thirty years ago. Like many of today's great scrapbookers, she was a child who loved to take pictures and have her nails polished and boss people around. The day she came up with the clever idea to create her first original scrapbook was the start of a beautiful pastime. Growing up, she had other hobbies too—ice-skating, baking, crocheting, doll-making, knitting, needle-pointing, quilting, sewing (pretty much all the skills I hope to acquire, cross my heart, before I die, even if it means sticking a knitting needle in my eye)—but she always especially loved taking pictures. Her first camera, a black box with a lens and a couple of levers, is now an antique, practically. Long ago she wrapped that special camera in tissue and tucked it safely away in a pink box and now nobody is allowed to hold it, even if all you wish to do is look at it, or pretend you want to sell it for her on eBay.

When she was a girl my sister was not satisfied to simply slip her photos into a preconstructed album; no, she was inspired to design her own layouts and pages. On her own, without examples or instructions, she took some of her photos and some of her notebook paper and created a charming little scrapbook. She still has that handmade treasure, complete with her original embellishment and comments and it is a wonderful thing. (Don't even think about asking her if you can hold it or pretend to sell it on eBay.)

It is such a darling piece of creative work that it makes sense to share with you the steps to creating one like it. So here you go, a step-by-step guide to creating my sister's first album:

1. Take a half dozen 11½" × 8" sheets of white, blue-lined notebook paper and fold each one into quarters.

2. Following the fold lines, use your father's good toenail scissors to cut the folded paper into four pages.

3. Using said scissors, carefully poke a small hole in the middle of each page. Starting at this small opening, cut an oval-, heart-, or triangle-shaped window in the first page and each subsequent page. Each shape should be large enough to frame the subject of your photo, but small enough so the

edge of the shape does not touch the edge of the paper.

4. Using a newly sharpened No. 2 pencil, punch a pencil-sized hole in the left-hand top corner of each page.

5. Apply Elmer's Glue generously to the back of your first page. Try to keep the glue away from the edge of the cut-out area and off of your fingers, as even a small drop can permanently smudge and possibly ruin your snapshot.

6. Place your photo on the page so the person in the photo can be seen through the cut-out shape.

7. Using your finger (or the file from your father's toiletries kit), smooth the glue *away* from the cut-out area. It cannot be stressed enough how damaging glue can be to your photos. Also, keep in mind, a little goes a long way. When the photo outside the framed area has dried fast to the paper, set page aside and repeat Step 5 until all of the pages have a photo attached.

8. Take a break. Get a fresh stick of gum. Then squeeze Elmer's Glue into your right hand's palm. Make certain you have enough to completely cover both of your palms. Once both your right and left palms are coated in glue, hold them apart, glue-side up, until dry. Be patient. Next, carefully peel

off the thin, flaky sheets of glue, which, if applied correctly, should resemble the shapes of your hands. Roll the dried glue into a wad or ball and continue rolling until the wad or ball of hardened glue is discolored and of no interest to anyone.

9. Get back to work. Line up all the newly created pages and feed a red piece of yarn through the holes you created in Step 4. Tie the ends of the yarn into a secure bow.

10. Using a blue pen, write evocative descriptions under each photo. For example, following my sister's example on the page that bears a photo of your mom relaxing in a hammock, write: "Mom cool as a clam with a baby in her youterus [*sic*]."

11. Design an eye-catching cover using colored markers. Create fancy letters that say: ME AND MY FAMILY!!!

It's your call, but if you decide to create a scrapbook like my sister's first scrapbook I would suggest you not use Elmer's Glue, since it is not to my knowledge photo-safe. Also, you're presumably an adult, so it makes sense to simply skip Step 8 altogether.

Well, after her first scrapbook was completed, my sister went on to follow her bliss and use her God-given gift to create subsequent scrapbooks (today, she has hundreds). Like all great scrapbookers' albums, hers are the products of continuous improvement and repeated investments of time and effort. She is a scrapaholic and she has reared two daughters who are scrapaholics too. One of them, maybe you know her, maybe you don't, is much like many of your children who were reared in a scrapbooking environment. From the time this niece was five you could put a pair of scissors in her hand and she would run toward whatever paper-cutting task was within reach. She took great pleasure in sitting at a table next to her mother as they cut out whatever it was they needed at the moment to create designs for their larger-than-life scrapbooks.

Now an adult, this niece creates artwork for large scrapbooking companies. When she's not working at designs for others she is creating scrapbooks of her own. I once sat next to her at an event at which there were fireworks. She was delighted by the show, which she viewed through one of her many Nikon lenses. When, a few days later, she showed me photos of the show, I was stupefied by the number of pictures I held. "These over here are the best shots," she said picking up an altogether different stack, which made me want to rush right out and buy one hundred shares of Kodak.

In any event, at any event, she was raised to be a scrapbooker's scrapbooker. Which is why, currently, this niece and her new husband, a young man who I must say has the most gorgeous eyes and smile I have ever seen, after fewer than twelve months of marriage already have on a shelf in their living room a dozen or so amazing memory books covering, in chronological order, their life together thus far. That is to say: Friendship; Courtship; Engagement; Bridal Showers; Bachelor Party (the slimmest album, by far—practically without photographs); Wedding Preparations; Wedding Day; Wedding Reception; and Honeymoon. Interspersed within these albums are bridal shower invitations, favors, and photos; samples of the wedding invitation (beautifully hand assembled, lettered, and embossed); and wedding cards and gift tags, along with ticket stubs and other memorabilia. In the meantime, this niece is completing their "Our First Year Together" scrapbook.

I tell you, children with at least one scrapbooking parent are likely to grow up to become scrapbook addicts too. Sure, they may be positively affected as a result of being part of a family where they had their own scrapbooks, but too bad they will need to work a second job to pay for their addiction.

CHAPTER 28

Hands-Off Scrapbooking

There are scrappers, and then there are *scrap*pers. There are scrappers who, though they are wont to deny it, will from time to time sit down to create a scrapbook page only to find themselves in another dimension—far off in a realm where nothing looks quite right, whatever that means. Surrounded by nonsense, they are paralyzed. They are paralyzed to the point of being unable or unwilling to lift a finger to complete a scrapbook page.

One of these very people is a person I know and love well, a person who looks up to me as an older sister since she is my younger sister and shorter than I. One day she was all set to scrapbook, when suddenly her efforts came to an abrupt stand-still. She just sat there for a painful moment looking down her nose at the photographs lying faceup on her dining room table. She finally announced she felt like scrapping these photos, but not in a good way. She wanted to gather them up in one fell swoop and trash them all. Sitting across the table from her, I had a responsibility as my sister's keeper to see her through this rough patch.

"How many scrapbookers does it take to change a light-bulb?" I playfully asked.

"Oh! Good *lord!*" she said, ignoring my riddle and pointing to a photograph of herself. "My hair! Tell me my hair has honestly never looked this ridiculous."

"Honestly?" I asked, trying to be kind without tainting my reputation for always being truthful even when, especially when, the truth hurts.

Before I could say a word she tore the photo in half and picked up another picture of herself standing outside of a hospital the day after her twins were born. "For crying out loud," she cried, "the camera added a good thirty pounds in this photo, and a chin! And where exactly is my neck?"

"The babies sure do look cute," I said.

Then she grabbed another photo and asked, "Is this me or is this not our mother in this picture?"

"Look at the shoes," I prompted.

"Oh! You're right, those are my shoes!" she bawled. "Why in the h-e-double-toothpick did I ever leave the house wearing those shoes?"

"A better question would be why you ever bought those shoes in the first place," I pointed out.

Next, she went on to pick on her children. Being the adoring aunt of these beautiful youngsters I will not repeat in writing what their mother said that day as she went through the most recent photos of her children. I will only say that she started in with something about how she should sue the unskilled loon who cuts her children's hair and ended with a cruel and sarcastic observation about her children's lack of poise, all of which left me thinking how like our mother this sister really is.

"Sometimes I can't believe my ears!" I told her.

"They do protrude, it's true," she shot back.

Anyway, before I could say something about how hair grows back and the sun comes out tomorrow, and her sons' braces will be coming off next month, she was talking to her photos: "Back you go, right back into the storage box where you belong, and no coming out until I say you can."

Then she picked up a finished scrapbook she had created for her daughter. It was a beautiful baby scrapbook, the very scrapbook I had moments before made a big fuss over because it was, frankly, adorable. It was just the sort of scrapbook that made me more determined than ever to create similar scrapbooks for my children. Suddenly, she began busily dismounting everything in this adorable scrapbook that she felt was worth saving. "Change of plans," she explained. "Today I focus on re-doing Erin's baby book, since that little sweetie deserves decent visual documentation of her first year, and as is quite obvious, this ridiculous scrapbook was put together before I really knew anything about coordinating photos with background paper!"

Thinking her behavior could not have been worse, I watched as she immediately proved me wrong when her youngest son, who was home from school because of a playground injury, came into the room. Seeing the scrapbooking supplies on the table he gleefully asked his mother if he might see his scrapbooks. She looked at him as if he had just walked across the room trailing clouds of gray toxic waste. "You know the rule, my love: No shower, no scrapbook. Go shower, use lots of soap on your hands, and then we'll talk about looking at your scrap-books," she said as she shooed him away.

"But Mom, I'm hungry! What's for lunch?" he said.

"Can you believe this kid?" she asked me before getting up and going into the kitchen.

She returned and handed her son a half-eaten bag of Fig Newtons. "Here you go, sweetie, enjoy! Enjoy these outside un-til I finish up in here."

When he complained she had given him Fig Newtons for breakfast, she calmly, but with a slight edge to her voice, re-minded him that this was—was it not?—her scheduled Scrap-booking Day, and the only way she was going to make the most of their lives was with his cooperation. Both her son and I looked baffled and a little appalled, so she went back into the kitchen and returned with a glass of milk and a Flintstone vita-min. "Here," she said, "now please, please, please, just go! Give me an hour without any more interruptions."

He started to point out that his mother knew he preferred the Fred vitamin, but stopped midsentence and dejectedly walked toward the back door—ignoring his scrapbooking mother's pre-occupied question: "Oh, and how's that head wound, little guy?"

CHAPTER 29

World Peace Through Scrapbooking

Yoo-hoo! **Paging all scrapbookers!** Grab your X-acto knives, pick up your glue guns, and arm yourself with *Chalk! Paper! Scissors!* It is time to create world peace! A task that, thankfully, is not near as daunting or as toilsome as it sounds, especially for those of you who have that delightful sense of purpose and humor for which scrapbookers are famous.

Just the other day, the idea to scrapbook the world's wars and woes away dawned on me while doing my morning reading. There on the back of a box of sugar-coated cereal I read: "To bring about peace, every person on earth must create something original." Naturally, my immediate thought was this: Scrapbookers are all about creating originals. Why not world peace? Why not enlist scrapbookers armed with their positive life-force, energy, originality, and creativity to bring about social and psychological change for the good of all nations and all people? [Editor: Does anybody have any idea what she is talking about?] I'm talking about World Peace, is what I'm talking about!

Sure, getting the citizens of the world to stop wanting each other dead will be a bit of an uphill battle, but scrapbookers have a unique way of getting things going and getting things done! Their dynamic energy, how-to savoir faire, and loving ways of approaching life may be the last hope for this mean old world. So join hands, won't you? It is time to scrap war and start scrappin'!

(If you just slapped your thigh and said, "Well, why not!" that's the spirit! You are definitely the type of peace-loving hobbyist this planet needs. If, on the other hand, you just rolled your eyes and said, "Don't be an idiot!" you are probably not a scrapbooker and one wonders what business you have reading this book in the first place and calling me an idiot in the second place. [Editor: Editor's prerogative, if not force of habit.] Well, this is exactly how family feuds that lead to world wars get started, so if you can't say something nice, go work for Halliburton.)

Back to peace on earth. Obviously, we—and by "we" I mean scrapbookers who feel war is not the answer—need to convince the world's leaders it is possible to reach out to other countries and develop a mutually rewarding relationship that lasts longer than the closing ceremonies of the Summer Olympics. To kick things off, scrapbookers from every nation could stage an all-night Peace Crop. As a rule, crops always include an abundance of friendship, a great deal of creative affirmation, and plenty of good food. In other words, the sort of things everybody in the world desires and many would kill for. If scrapbookers could combine their positive energy, enthusiasm, and creativity to bring about wholeness and happiness, then surely the peoples of the world would come to see each other as not so bad after all. If you have ever been part of a scrapbooking group you know there is a process that turns strangers into friends, a process that involves talking and sharing and smiling at photos of one another's children. In that moment, or month, or whatever it takes, when you make a scrapbook for a stranger, that stranger becomes a friend. The result would be forgiveness, acceptance, even appreciation. As an added incentive, everyone goes home with complimentary scrapbook supplies and Peace Treats. I think this could be a huge shove in the right direction. [Editor: This indeed is what I would give her if she were within shoving distance.]

Seriously, these Peace Crops would be a riot! Then, to keep the ball rolling, scrapbookers will be drafted (although most scrappers I know would gladly volunteer, especially if it meant a little time away from the kids) to complete Special Service Projects like creating "Friendship Scrapbooks," which would then be sent to foreign lands in need of aid (i.e., wherever bellicose citizens can be found repeatedly rushing out into the streets, chanting angry nonsense, burning flags, and throwing devices designed to inflict injury). What might these teeth-gnashing mobs of individuals possibly need besides reparative dental work? For starters, they need kindhearted scrapbookers to demonstrate there are better things to do in life than protest. If we're going to eliminate hatred and fear, our best bet is to use our best weapons: originality, kindness, humor, and creativity.

Our so-called enemies will be so pleased with their scrapbook supplies and so touched by our efforts that all thoughts of war will fade like photos on alkaline paper.

Inspired by our caring and relieved to be trading war-torn borders for torn scrapbook borders, they would in all likelihood and in all neighborhoods become determined to join us in forging peace together, forever. [Editor: She's mad, you know.] Call me mad, for I am mad at myself for not thinking of this idea sooner. By giving others a completed scrapbook, you make them happy for a day. By teaching others to scrapbook, you make them happy for a lifetime! And, as an added bonus, you develop your own creativity and intelligence, stop the madness, and prevent nuclear warfare from messing up your kid's chance of going to college.

Historically, peace on earth has not been embraced by our world's leaders—or many of our world's followers, for that matter. If history has taught us anything, it's that war has bombed. As you will recall from Tolstoy's *War and Peace* (a book that—although I never read beyond the first few chapters given there were too many confusing names, French phrases, and battle scenes for my taste—is judged by many to be a pretty decent read), when people are hungry or feel nobody likes them, everybody hates them, they will not go eat worms. No, they will become warmongers.

Lord knows, we've given war our best shot, now it's time to try something that works wonders. Far more cheering and possible is peace if we:

1. Change the U.N. to the F.U.N. Give the United
   Nations a new name along with an actual reason for

existing. Assign scrapbookers, renamed F.U.N.
Officials, to every single delegate from every nation.
Note: Nations with dictatorships would be assigned
extra scrapbookers along with whoopee cushions.

2. Create and distribute bumper stickers with the
following messages:
SHOOT PICTURES, NOT PEOPLE
PICTURE PERFECT PEACE
SCRAPPERS WITHOUT BORDERS
STAMP OUT WAR
CHARMS NOT ARMS

3. Establish institutions that promote peace. For
example, right next to West Point, build the
Scrapbooking College of Collage to educate and
inspire the Peace Croppers of the future.

You might be asking yourself: Who's going to pay for this
scrap-roots effort? Answer: The United States government,
that's who. In the name of peacekeeping, our congress coughed
up $56 billion in April 2003 and another $72 billion in November 2003, and is currently in the process of spending an additional $25 billion. The total amounts to over $150 billion! Just
think of the paper, albums, embellishments, cameras, copiers,
scanners, glue, food, shelter, health care, and education these
billions could buy along with a shot at turning our many enemies into our friends.

World peace through scrapbooking may seem like an impossible dream right now, but think back to when creating a
scrapbook also seemed an impossibility for you. Let's just take

it one day at a time until the world is on the same page. Yes, there will be the occasional scrap now and then, but it can quickly be turned into a harmony-keeping crop.

So soldier on, you peace-loving scrapbookers. To paraphrase Mr. Victor-Marie (Marie? Ha! Girl's name!) Hugo: Not all the armies in the world can stop an idea whose time has come. I pray you see the sense in this idea because if you don't, maybe someone should sit you down and slap you silly.

C H A P T E R   30

Coming to Terms with Scrapbooking

Think back to when your first scrapbook was nothing more than a pile of slightly out-of-focus photos and a blank pseudo-leather album waiting to be slapped together. Sure, it was a dull and relatively wretched time when the only stickers in your life said "Chiquita," the only fonts were baptismal, and fiber was just a worthwhile ingredient in your breakfast cereal. Back then, before modern-day scrapbooking, "die-cut" was shorthand for "make my hair look gorgeous" and "embellishment" was code for a guilt-free way of stretching the truth through your teeth.

Then, little by little, you started throwing around scrap-booking terms like "layouts," "scoring," "top loading," "gripping," and "translucent vellum"—terms your husband was disappointed to learn had nothing to do with spending time alone with him. Before long your vocabulary expanded to include "rotating ball-bearing disc," "cutters," "power punch," and "Shrinky Dink"—at which time your spouse became grateful scrapbooking did *not* include time alone with him.

And now, look at you. Phrases like "design theory," "foundational techniques," and "doodle dotters" roll off your tongue like ink out of a liquid pen. Unless, of course, you are a scrapbooking novice, in which case you may want to rip (since you do not yet own a craft knife) this chapter from this book and carry it around in your wallet as a handy reference guide. If this book does not belong to you—say, for example, it belongs to the public library—then you should think twice about taking any of its pages without first getting permission. Maybe look around for a copy machine, but whatever you do (let your conscience be your guide) just be sure to use this guide of descriptive scrapbooking words and expressions. For what it's worth, even if you have been scrapbooking for years, the list below will benefit experienced and inexperienced scrapbookers alike, so nobody goes away empty-headed. (I know what you're thinking, and you're welcome!)

So without further Un-do glue, here, in glowing terms, are all the scrapbooking definitions you will ever need to know:

SCRAPAPATHY: A rare but sluggish feeling with regards to completing a scrapbooking project. Ex.: "Her *scrapapathy* led to one too many aperitifs before dinner."

SCRAPLIFTING: When one scrapper takes another scrapper's idea or tool without asking permission. Ex.: "Thinking nobody would be the wiser, she went about *scraplifting* border ideas from other scrappers."

SCARFBOOKER: Rapid snacking rather than scrapping. Ex.: "The scrapbooker sat down to pleat paper with pizzazz, but ended up eating a pizza instead—which left her feeling like a *scarfbooker.*"

SCRAPROOKIE: A person who is new to scrapbooking. Ex.: "She was such a *scraprookie* that she used Elmer's Glue and phrases like, 'Anybody mind if I smoke?' "

SCRAP BOOING: The sound used by experienced scrapbookers to express dissatisfaction or contempt. Ex.: "The croppers started *scrap booing* when asked by a scraprookie, 'Anybody mind if I smoke?' "

QUILLING: A technique where thin strips of colored paper are rolled into decorative shapes. Ex.: "She sang while rolling strips of black and yellow paper, *quilling* bees softly with her song."

PHOTOGAFFE: A picture-taking faux pas. Ex.: "It was a *photogaffe* to take pictures of her husband during his root canal surgery."

TEMP PLATE: Any flat surface temporarily used to hold one's snack food when scrapping. Ex.: "There was so little clear space on her scrapbooking table, she used some cardstock as a temp plate for her chocolate éclair."

LAMINATION LAMENTATION: The woe a scrapper experiences if she is unable to successfully cover something with a translucent plastic protector. Ex.: "She *lamented* her lack of *lamination* skill."

SANDING: The process of distressing paper and fresh manicures. Ex.: "After scraplifting the idea, she was caught roughing up her page border using a *sanding* technique."

SHABBY CHIC: You, after an all-night scrapbooking workshop. Ex.: "After cropping like mad for eight hours straight, everything, including you, starts looking *shabby chic*."

CHICLET: An emergency embellishment; not to be confused with "Chick Lit," a Chiclet has permanent artistic value. Ex.: "Desperate to complete the scrapbook layout before she returned home, she used the never-been-chewed *Chiclets* in her purse to create a border."

SCRAPLESS GOWN: What one might wear to a fancy crop. Ex.: "Her beautifully beaded *scrapless gown* was perfect social wear."

CROPHOBIA: The fear of scrapping anything that looks too complicated and appears to be beyond one's artistic abilities. Ex.: "People suffering from severe *crophobia* often will resort to merely *writing* about scrapbooking."

SCRAPPER SNOB: Anyone who is better at scrapbooking than you, and knows it. Ex.: "She turned into a total *scrapper snob* when her layout was featured in a craft magazine."

DO-GOODERS: Scrapper snobs who attend crop parties where they agree to complete the host's scrapbooks in exchange for her gratitude, food, foot rubs, and prize giveaways. Ex.: "Always eager to be the center of attention, the scrapper snobs enjoyed their roles as *do-gooders.*"

PAGE PRIG: A scrapbooker who gets snippety when offered a page suggestion. Ex.: "When someone joked her layout was about as attractive as a piece of scrap metal, the *page prig* responded curtly."

SCRAP-LOOKING: The always popular activity of viewing another's scrapbook. Ex.: "Unable to create scrapbooks for herself, she made cutting remarks as she was *scrap-looking* at memory books belonging to her sister."

Those are all the terms we have time for today. Many more scrapbooking words or word combinations are out there, which made it a tricky business deciding which particular ones to include here. It was hit and miss, let me tell you! Some essential terms didn't make the cut because, frankly, they are too common and I just assumed you are not someone who wants the obvious explained. I mean, why bore you to tears? Why tell you something you already know? I don't want you yawning, I really don't.

CHAPTER 31

The Grim Scrapper

Much as we all wish it were not so, and miserable though it is to consider, now and then even a fun-loving scrapper may find herself sitting in the gloom of night, gripped by an intense loathing of her existence. By "an intense loathing of her existence" I simply mean an unsettled feeling like a little gray cloud bumping up against her thoughts. You know, the type you get when experiencing water retention, or when something as insignificant as gravity gets you down.

Sometimes this gray cloud means we're mourning something as evasive as our lost youth. On occasion it is nothing more than a thwarted whim, a dab of depression, or disorientation brought on by too much chocolate (or not nearly enough). Then there are the other times when it is more serious, more a halfhearted panic that the apocalypse is just around the corner and Death himself is rappin' at the door. Something like:

DEATH: [knock-knock!]

YOU: Whoa! Who is there?

DEATH: Yo! My name is Death, also known as the grim rapper.

You! Your time be up, there ain't nothin' left to scrap, dear.

A-*ha*! Uh *ha*!

[Editor: Eye-yi-yi! This, my friends, is what happens when a middle-aged white woman whose favorite radio program is NPR's *Wait, Wait . . . Don't Tell Me!* tries to write rap.]

Fine. So anyway, for the sake of moving on, let's just say that, like it or not, from time to time some of us feel sad. We'll call it that time of the month and leave it at that. Sad is what a scrapbooking friend, who calls herself "Sunny," was feeling recently when I went knocking on her door.

Sunny seemed discouraged; she thought all was lost. So I suggested she count her many blessings. She, however, refused. So, rather than name them for her, one by one, I suggested she continue watching daytime television. This was, not to brag, excellent advice—because that's where she was, sitting on the couch watching a self-help talk show, when her salvation arrived. He arrived in the form of a positive-attitude expert who shared with the viewing audience the best pick-me-up advice ever. Sunny was encouraged by the expert's recommendation to chase away her blues by doing something that has in the past been a source of happiness. Sunny loved to scrapbook. Now, at the time, she did not have the energy to scrapbook; in fact, she lacked the energy to brush her hair or the cupcake crumbs from her mouth. Yet the advice to get going was enough to get Sunny thinking in a new light.

Still nursing her nerves and feeling close to comfortless, deprived as she was of her easy chair and flat-screen TV at home,
Sunny found herself sitting in a scrapbooking class pushing vigorously at her cuticle skin so as to avoid having to make eye contact
with the other scrappers seated at the table. Suddenly, a vivacious
woman walked right up, smiled warmly, then leaned in to whisper
in Sunny's ear, "Excuse me, dear, I always sit here, so scoot!"

Bewildered by the odd request and bothered by the
woman's glue gun—which was poking Sunny in the ribs—she
sat there stunned until the woman hissed, "Now."

Sensing this scrapbooker was as stable as a teeter-totter,
Sunny moved to another seat, then nervously tapped her heels together and wished she were home. (Home watching *America's Most
Wanted*, where she felt sure she would see the face of the woman
who had come unglued when she saw Sunny sitting in her chair.)

Just in time, the scrapbook instructor arrived and said,
"Welcome, my scrap-happy friends. I am a scrapbook teacher
but more than that I am an instructor of life, a bringer of light, a
teller of truth."

As she went on to explain the wisdom of scrapbooking and
how it leads to deeper love, better health, perfect kindness, uni-
versal peace, a clearer complexion, and material wealth, Sunny
and the other scrappers nodded in agreement. "You, my fellow
scrapbookers, are called to be the Keepers of Treasures, the
Makers of Memories, yes, the Savers of Lives!"

Next, the instructor asked the class a question: "What is going on in your world and in yourself that prevents you from being serene and really productive at scrapbooking?"

"I'd say," Sunny said, unaware the question was rhetorical,
"that's for me to know and you to find out."

"Well, what I've found out," the master scrapbooker replied, "is one must constantly pursue photographic pleasures while counting her blessings; this is a passionate scrapper's true life-affirming way."

After a short period of photo-gluing, or, as it was called that evening, "scrapper bonding," the teacher complimented the class on their stick-to-itiveness, then moved on to decorative edges. "It's all a matter of personal preference, how you like your edge," she said. "I like mine scrambled, or boiled," said Sunny, suppressing a laugh.

Too soon the class was over. But before they left, the teacher reminded her students, "Remember, scrapbooking is fun! And easy!" Every scrapper nodded and smiled wisely, including Sunny. Moments later the woman who had earlier told Sunny to scoot was standing in front of her. "Forgive me?" she asked, then handed over her glue gun. "Glue unto others." Then, with a suitably contrite look she turned and was gone.

To Sunny's delight the gray cloud was gone too, as she walked out of the class chanting, "Yo, my name is Sunny, but you can call me scrapper!"

So you see? All's well that ends with a good bit of scrapping and rapping. The next time you're down or lonely, get out! Wise up! Go to a scrapbooking class! OK? Got it? Good. That's a rap.

[Editor's note: Duh, none of this happened.]

Yo!

CHAPTER 32

Tick Tock, the Crop Is Locked

There is a class war going on in America, and I fear it's only going to get worse—as long as scrapbookers are forced to fight over the limited space in crop workshops.

Yes, we need more scrapbooking classes and we need them *yesterday*. I really could have used them last month, when I went online to sign up for a few classes offered as part of a scrapbook convention and came away emptyhanded, my simple needs unmet. I had no desire whatsoever to try something so advanced as turning watermarked paper into divine marbleized paper, nor was I anywhere near ready to dress up cardstock with spray paint, bleach, uranium, or any other uniquely fabulous albeit dangerous technique, regardless of the splendid results. No, all I was looking for was a class or two that would allow me to walk right in off the street, sit down, and then six hours later walk out with a finished product in my hands. So that was really the only criterion I had for choosing a class—the promise of instant scrapbook success. That and free samples. Also, I wanted fast, cheap, and good without having to choose two out of the three.

The first workshop in the lineup "invited the Beginner Scrapper to jump right in for some *fun*-tastic tactics and techniques and new ideas that are sure to please!" Pleased already, I jumped right in with both feet and typed in all the pertinent registration information. Expecting a three-exclamation-point confirmation to promptly appear, I was surprised and disappointed when, instead, up popped the apologetic words: "Sorry, class full!" *Poop*.

Not one to be easily dissuaded or distressed (so early in the game, anyway) I read on and discovered a workshop promising ". . . sixty minutes of emotional and teary-eyed sharing time, while learning how to scrapbook life's most sacred places and feelings." Sacred places and feelings? Count me out. I'm self-conscious about sharing my height and weight, let alone my sacred places and feelings. Also, I've been accused of contriving sacred feelings. When I gaze deeply at the beauty of the infinite night sky, or lovingly into the astonishing eyes of my children, I am the type who gets black-hole feelings, the kind that lead me to ask profound questions like, "Is that pinkeye you've got there?"

So you see, I would have trouble publicly getting into the spirit of a sacred workshop. Still, I decided to try, but again the class was full. *Crop!*

The next class I attempted to sign up for asked the question: "Are you color challenged?" "Who's not?" strikes me as a better question. Still, it depends on what hues we're talking about. I've had my share of clashing colors and tainted tints. I've been burnt by orange, shocked by pink, even jaded by green. So my colors are primarily red, yellow, and blue—which, if not exactly challenging, are sometimes too bold and cheerful for my pages. This class description promised to teach me to "create beautiful backgrounds using stamps, inks, and sponges while learning a variety of titillating techniques to make scrapbook pages come alive!"

I decided I could live with these living colors. Except for the fact the class was full. Sorry. *Sorry my acid-free foot*!

For crying out loud! Now I was starting to really, really need a class. I continued down the long list until I read the words: "Are you ready to start a scrapbook but don't know where to begin?" Ready or not, I certainly needed to know whether the class was full. Which it was.

The next workshop in the lineup asked if I was willing to "experience page ideas that would surely stagger the imagination." Of course, I wished to be staggered—and I would be, if I were to find out that the class had room for me. But of course those hopes were dashed. *What the h-e-double-gluestick*?

The next workshop description asked if I was ". . . ready to learn from the greatest scrap experts?"

"Does a bear scrap in the woods?" I asked out loud. Sure, I was more than ready to learn from the experts! To show just how ready I immediately attempted to sign up for this exercise in creativity and within seconds was sent the message I longed not to hear: *Sorry, class full.*

"Scrapbooking is fun! Scrapbooking is easy!" claimed the lead-in to the next advertised workshop. "Much easier than you think, and we are here to prove it!" I wanted them to prove it— oh, how I wanted them to prove it. *Sorry, class full.*

It cannot be underestimated how rude those three words

started to sound. Sorry, class full. Sorry, class full. Another class description explained how if I gave them $20 and my attention for an hour they would "empower mixing and matching, pulling and lifting, pushing and punching, tying and crimping, layering and lettering" skills to add excitement to my scrapbook pages. I believe that they would have, but I'll never know since the class was, sorry, full.

Sorrowful is what I was from the moment I realized I was out of choices. As I perused the remaining classes on the list I realized they were far too esoteric for me and intended for only the rare and gifted few who knew the secret handshake and owned their own rotating ball-bearing disc. So, as much as I wanted— nay, needed—to create a memory album that "no one would be able to resist opening," and despite my longing to "see for myself how easy it is to design fabulous layouts," and regardless of my growing desire to apply "some easy-to-apply workable strategies for getting my scrapbooking life organized," I was plain out o' luck. Every single beginner's class was closed to the latecomers of the world. By "latecomers" I mean anybody who, like me, had waited until the event was only three months away. Obviously, several months too late to do me any good at all.

As a last resort I asked my sweet niece if she would let me go to some of the classes she had successfully signed up for months ahead of me. Selfishly she refused my request to share any of her classes. In fact, she laughed in my face before saying she would rather give up a kidney than give up her place in a single scrapbook workshop.

Well, I didn't need a kidney, so I was left with nothing.

CHAPTER 33

Scrapbookers' Rights

A slapdash analysis of scrapbooking, which is what this book is if you think about it, must include, sooner or later, an unbiased look at the places where thousands of people gather periodically to discuss, trade, purchase, sell, demonstrate, and celebrate scrapbooking products and ideas.

So, with all sorts of expectations, I walked into an enormous convention center where a huge extravaganza was in full swing. Immediately I was disoriented and overwhelmed by the sheer energy and oddity of the gathering. I put my hand over my name badge, which was over my heart, and stood there wondering why there were women wearing thongs and high heels at this scrapbook convention. I just never thought of scrapbookers as the types to wear thongs in public, but there they were, swaying their hips and swinging their elbows flashing perpetual smiles as they gracefully pointed at shiny sports cars. It was only when I asked directions to the "Creating Keepsakes" booth that I was made to understand that I was in the wrong convention hall.

After leaving the Auto Show and walking north, I found the scrapbooking convention in full swing. If you have never had the chance to attend one of these extravaganzas let me tell you right off the bat, they are not for the weak of heart. There were rows upon rows of colorful, snazzy, eye-catching displays, booths filled with the latest and greatest scrapbooking creations, and people greeting guests like long-lost friends. You would be hard-pressed to find another place in town where so much hugging was going on. Even if you choose not to embrace the friendly people, you'll want to embrace their free products. Which is why, let me also tell you, you're going to need a large bag or small shopping cart to carry all the complimentary paper samples, stickers, T-shirts, pens, photographs, and treats being handed out.

Conventions often feature famous people in the industry, and this convention followed that convention by inviting some of today's scrapbooking greats. These famous scrapbookers were graciously signing autographs and posing for photographs, while a crowd of admirers tried not to fawn or grovel. I finally got near enough to one Big Name to shout, "You're the best!" She looked right at me and smiled in that appreciative way that fooled me into believing it was the first time she had ever had such a genuine compliment. Others were going up to her and saying things like, "I adore you!" and "I named my daughter after you!" but she remained nonplussed and humble.

One well-known "scrapbooking queen" was scheduled to give a lecture entitled "Scrapbookers' Rights," so I made a beeline for the room where she was scheduled to speak. The first thing I noticed as I sat down within an arm's reach of a jelly bean–filled bowl was that there were bowls of jelly beans everywhere. The next thing I noticed was the so-called scrapbooking queen wearing a timid expression, beige slacks, a pink sweater set, and a single strand of pearls. Tuck a pencil behind her ear and she was the spitting image of my second grade teacher.

As people filed in, found their seats, and scooped up handfuls of jelly beans, the instructor stood at the lectern looking cheerfully around the room. Finally, in a sweet voice, she invited attendees to please take a seat. Then she transformed herself into a fiery, yet civil (rights), leader. First she dropped her smile and then her shoulders, clasped her hands behind her back, and trudged across the stage, looking pretty serious for a scrapper.

"Stand with me, sisters," she suddenly said. Her voice was so commanding and powerful, it caused everyone to jump to her feet.

"Now join me in raising your hands in the air." Everybody put her hands up.

"Now wave your hands in the air, wave them like you just don't care!"

Hands were flailing to and fro, jelly beans were flying.

"Okay, now put your left hand down, put your right hand up, I said, put your left hand down. Good, now repeat after me," she continued. "I, state your name [the roomful of women said "I," then simultaneously stated their names], have the right to scrapbook whenever, whatever, and wherever I feel like it."

The women repeated this, after which the leader said, "Please, be seated."

I, however, was the only one who obeyed. As I sat there

noticing the recent weight gain in my thighs, everyone else—
being true scrappers—broke into astonishing applause. They
slapped the palms of their hands together and whistled like
longshoremen until the speaker requested they settle down.
She then flipped on an overhead projector and displayed these
words against the front wall: "Scrapbookers are entrusted with
priceless treasures."

Well, obviously. This group of scrapbookers was a flashy
crowd. I had not seen so many bejeweled women named Tiffany
since attending my previous workshop, which I believe was
called, "Scrapbooking Objects for Those for Whom Money is No
Object."

As it turned out, the "priceless treasures" to which the instructor was referring were, in fact, scrapbooks. "It is our right, it
is our duty, it is our special calling," she said, "to create photo
albums that will be treasured by our children, our children's
children, our great-grandchildren, and so on."

"Yes!" Several women called out. "Yes, forever and ever!" A
woman sitting directly behind me called out as other scrapbookers vigorously nodded their heads in total agreement.

"Future generations have entrusted us to preserve treasures, create scrapbooks, build up a photo fortune, if you will!"

"I will!" more than a few women declared.

"Creating a scrapbook is a highly honorable, desirable, and
completely selfless contribution!" the leader loudly exclaimed
while punctuating her remarks by pounding her closed fist
against her chest.

"That is why—and correct me if I'm wrong—that is why I believe scrapbookers have inalienable rights!"

"Absolutely!" "Undeniably!" "Indisputably!" "Incontrovertibly!" "Irrefutably!" "No shit!" women around me shouted. That, or words close to these words that I just came up with after looking up the word "absolutely" in a thesaurus.

"You have the right to remain silently scrapbooking for as long as you please for as long as it takes to complete a memory book! This may be five hours, five days, it may be five months, it may take you the better part of a year, but nobody in his right mind will prohibit your creative license."

More loud applause as the instructor began pacing back and forth across the front of the room. "Whenever inspiration hits, and hit you it will, you have the right to scrapbook. Even if there are dishes stacked in the sink. Even if there are socks unfolded in the dryer. Even if there are unmade beds or children crying to be fed, you shall not deny yourself the right to scrapbook when inspiration strikes."

Once again all the women were on their feet, stomping and clapping to beat the band. Did I mention there was a live band? There was. A four-piece band repeatedly striking just the right chord with this crowd.

"Sisters, you have the right to your own scrapbooking space. This may be the entire basement; it may be your dining room, your half of the bedroom, or the kitchen table! You take out a home improvement loan if needs be because you have the right to a room of your own!" she said to much wild applause. First her own, before others joined in. "It's your right!" she emphasized, once again using the pounding-fist-on-chest gestures, which were starting to look as if they hurt a little. Definitely this woman did not have breast implants.

As the group settled back into their chairs I reached for more candy and smiled slyly to myself as it dawned on me what was going on here. We were being filmed on a hidden camera. This had to be some highly dramatized reality craft show. I started looking around the room for the television crew but all I found instead were hundreds of ladies with cameras around their necks madly taking notes while sitting on the edge of their folding chairs.

The instructor continued. "In whatever manner you see fit, even if it means throwing a fit, you have the right to peaceably assemble to crop, scrap, stamp, and emboss to your heart's content.

"You have the right to create pages that reflect your unique creativity. If not now, when? If not you, who?"

Loud, appreciative applause and hoots.

"You have the right to child-free scrap time!"

Louder applause and catcalls.

"You have the right to guilt-free, hassle-free, buy-two-get-one-free scrap time!"

Frenzied clapping and jumping up and down.

"And make no mistake," she said in a calmer, more serious voice, "you have the right to make mistakes! You're only human after all!"

Light questioning laughter followed by the audience members wincing in unison.

"Most importantly," she emphasized, "you must celebrate the glorious being creating the treasures—you! And you! And you! And you—all of you!" The instructor pointed her finger randomly around the room at several individuals, but not at me, which was disappointing and a relief at the same time.

"You have every right, every reason, to include yourself in every scrapbook you create," she said, as women dabbed tears from their eyes and I reached for more jelly beans. "Your photographic image may not always be included, but your distinctive creativity, your unique scrapbooking style will leave your distinct mark as sure as your signature.

"You have the right to use whatever you want in your scrapbooks; anything you please! You may place as many or as few photos per page as you deem appropriate. You have the right to purchase a scrapbook item for no other reason than it brings out the colors in your eyes. Remember, if you don't buy it, somebody else will.

"You have the right to socialize with other scrapbookers!

"Furthermore, you have the right to do nothing more than snack and socialize at a scrapbook retreat," the instructor proclaimed. "It's your party and you can crop if you want to—or not!"

Curiously, I was the only person to whistle and clap at this particular comment, so the instructor hurried on.

"In conclusion, say it loudly and say it proudly: You're a scrapper and you know it—clap your hands! You're a scrapper and you know it—clap your hands!"

The band started playing; everybody joined in, "You're a scrapper and you know it—clap your hands! You're a scrapper and you know it, and you've got the rights, so really show it! You're a scrapper and you know it—clap your hands!"

Immediately the room was filled with flying jelly beans, thunderous applause, and wild, happy music, and all felt right in the world.

Applause, applause, applause. These were happy people, these scrappers with rights.

CHAPTER 34

Scrapbooking Rules

The scrapbookers I know are a rule-bound bunch who would do well to consider the words of Thomas A. Edison, who said, "Hell, there are no rules here—we're trying to accomplish something."

Here are some other scrapbooking rules, axioms, and truths worth considering. Take comfort in them if you'd like. Or ignore them. It matters little to a rebel like me.

1. There is no burden that an hour's worth of scrapbooking won't lighten.

2. Without a touch of madness, there is no great scrapbooking.

3. Successful scrapbooking is 1 percent inspiration, 89 percent perspiration, and 10 percent snack food.

4. Strive for page completion, not perfection.

5. Scrapbooking's vitality lies in its creativity and originality.

6. You can attain immortality through scrapbooking, especially if you never dye.

7. Scrapbooking is a million ideas whose time has come.

8. Genius may have its limitations, but bad taste does not.

9. Nurture your family with good meals and great scrapbooks to ensure future greatness.

10. Five out of six scrapbookers are addicts.

11. Every great scrapbook must include laughter.

12. No act of scrapbooking, no matter how small, is ever wasted.

13. If you want people to be happy, make them a scrapbook.

14. A woman travels the world in search of meaning and then returns home to scrapbook it.

15. Being featured in a scrapbook reminds a child who she or he is and might become.

16. To avoid scrapbooking is to avoid life.

17. Scrapbookers do not live in the past so much as the past lives on in their scrapbooks.

18. There is no cure for scrapbooking but to scrapbook more.

19. Above all else, scrapbooking is the gift of happy memories.

20. Real scrapbooking is a self-improvement course that lasts a lifetime.

So as we take joy in scrapbooking, may we remember there's no wrong or right, no hard and fast rules when in comes to creating a page.

CHAPTER 35

True Lives of Scrapbookers

Some people in my family—and I am one of them—have never completed a decent scrapbook. We know in our bones scrapbooking is vital. We wait for creativity to flow. But still our measly attempts sort of suck. Sometimes—that is to say, times when we are scrapbooking together—one of my talented scrapbooking sisters and I will have a conversation that reminds me of those two dogs from that little novella where one dog, a mutt, tries to come up with a hat to impress another dog, a poodle, as it happens, and the mutt keeps asking the poodle, "Do you like my hat?" and the poodle always candidly replies, "I do not!" and then there's this unvarying exchange: "Good-bye! *Good-bye!*" Eventually, after many failed attempts to please the poodle, the mutt comes up with an outlandish hat that the poodle actually likes and the mutt looks delightedly smug. I am always so delighted when I have a page that my sister (the poodle) likes, but usually we just end up saying "Good-bye! *Good-bye!*"

We rationalize, we justify, we do our best to appear normal around our siblings who are scrapbookers. This is why I always experience a little relief when I talk with someone who has never successfully cropped anything in her life. For example, not so long ago I was chatting with a glass-half-empty sort of friend who started going on about why she has yet to create a single scrapbook. As she recited the all-too-familiar excuses (the very ones I always use) it occurred to me that just because I am sick and tired of hearing these excuses does not mean everybody is. There are plenty of people who, having never used a single one of these excuses, may find them interesting— useful even—in that way that makes a person feel superior. This gave me the bright idea to write a detailed if misconstrued account of why some people, particularly this friend, are not scrapbookers.

Then, on top of that great idea, I had another even better idea, which was to ask my nonscrapping friend to write an account of why she herself has failed to create a single book of photographic memories. Knowing full well how excruciating and time-consuming self-absorbed writing can be, I promised my friend anonymity if she promised to convey clearly and concisely, in her own words, saving me the burden of conveying clearly and concisely, in my own words, why she has never created a scrapbook. She kindly agreed to do her best and, well, sometimes your best isn't good enough. But what she came up with was nearly as good as anything I could have come up with, so who am I to complain? It would have been nice, however, if what she wrote was the slightest bit interesting.

Here is what she was willing to share with me via an e-mail:

Like I'm always telling my mother, the reasons I don't have any scrapbooks yet are personal, complicated, and, not to be rude, but none of her business. Since you asked, though, I gave it some more serious thought and I must say right up front that I am unsure whether I really *want* to make scrapbooks. I feel uncertain as to whether I'd even be a good scrapper. Sure, I like other people's scrapbooks, but when I'm around them for more than a few hours, I can't wait to hand over their scrapbooks and head home.

Contrary to popular belief, not everybody is cut out for scrapbooking. When I think about the huge time commitment, the expense, the sleep deprivation, the relentless responsibility—well, I just have all sorts of reservations.

Still, the facts are undeniable. I'm at that age when all my friends already have scrapbooks or are creating scrapbooks, and I've really got to hand it to them, they have done a wonderful job. Their scrapbooks are adorable and I'd be lying if I claimed to never think about having my own. Sometimes when I look at other scrapbookers happily carrying their bundles of supplies, dressing up their photographs, or talking about getting together with other young scrapbookers, my eyes fill with tears. Why them and not me? I feel like crying.

Maybe I could just start with baby steps. Perhaps keep a journal this weekend; see how that plays out.

Then if the journaling goes without any major mishaps, I could start planning a real scrapbook. I mean, who doesn't want scrapbooks around to comfort them when they are old?

Well, that's about it. I hope you can use this in your book about scrapbooking.

Now let me ask you a question, Wendy: Why are you even writing a book? Speaking of which, who's going to read this book of yours? [Editor: A good question if ever there was one.] I'm telling you, call the telemarketing company about that part-time job I mentioned last week.

Your pal in weirdness,

[signed by anonymous friend]

Naturally, I ignored my friend's unpleasant questions and, instead, congratulated myself on my acute ability to convince this particular person, who is not even a scrapbooker, to contribute to this book about scrapbooking!

Next, I went out and successfully rounded up a few more acquaintances [Editor: Which is to say, imaginary friends.] and offered them the same deal of anonymity in exchange for their personal, True Life scrapbook experiences. Their stories of success, failure, happiness, and brushes with fame and death are found on the pages to follow.

CHAPTER 36

True Lives of Scrapbookers #1: Camera Shy

[Author's note: For many years, nobody knew why, there was a nice, normal woman who refused be photographed. Not in a group, not from a distance, not in a box, not with a fox. Not for love or money would she allow her picture to be taken. She would show her displeasure if you even pretended to take her picture. If you actually took her picture, she would take your camera and destroy the film and, it goes without saying, the moment. Then, just last summer, this same camera-shy friend began posing like a celebrity. "What gives?" I asked. Well, so intriguing was her answer that I, with open arms, invited her to write about her complete turnaround.]

They say the camera never lies. But I say it sure can distort the truth. As proof let me tell you I am not now nor was I ever, in my opinion, an unattractive person, yet a good part of my life has been plagued by bad snapshots and the annoying realization that my photographic images never measured up to the mental images I carried around of myself. Photogenically speaking, I was unfortunate—which is probably why my mother always recorded my age in dog years on the back of the few pictures of me she saved.

Until recently, there were only four photos from my past actually worth keeping. Four candid shots that capture forever a younger, more innocent, more spontaneous me. These black-and-white pictures bring back cherished memories of a very special day, a day of walking down the aisle with anticipation; of lifting the veil (or curtain, or whatever you want to call it); waiting for the first flash; smiling timidly at the second; happily grinning for the third; going cross-eyed for the last flash; then pacing with self-conscious expectation before carefully removing the still-damp strip of four photos the moment they dropped into sight. Ah, sweet are the childhood memories. Next to being right there for a blue-light special, a better time could not be had at Kmart.

Otherwise and photo-wise I had no luck. The camera always zoomed in on the fact that I lack a good side. That is why, up until recently, whenever anyone pointed a camera in my direction, I would shout something instructive such as, "Damn! Don't shoot!" or "No photo, you idiot!"

Sometimes the obnoxious person with the camera would simply laugh and mistakenly assume I was just playing around, often resulting in a scuffle and, invariably, somebody getting their feelings hurt or their zoom lens broken. You know, we've all been there. At least you privacy-seeking celebrities have, and those of us who are not in the least photogenic.

Maybe I was vain, plain and simple. Or maybe it had something to do with my veins, the protruding varicose variety. The last time a size-8 swimsuit was stretched over the size-14 portion of my middle-aged body, my young child kept nervously glancing at the bumpy purple veins on my legs. Finally he asked—blurted, actually—"Are you going to die?" I assured him they were only for show, like the tattoos of insects and flowers on the legs of many of the younger mothers at the pool that day. Looking mostly unconvinced, yet willing to support my delusion, he pointed to one of the more pronounced veins on my right shin and shouted out, "My mommy has a purple snake on her leg!" What a pity I did not know then what I know now: Never have children.

Ha ha! I'm mostly kidding, but I'm quite serious about how much I now, at long last, enjoy smiling for the camera. Now, thanks to a few tricks of the scrapbooking trade, I can crop, snip, and photo-tint my way to a better-looking version of me using those scrapbooking tools available wherever fine scrapbooking supplies are sold. Like the plastic surgeon I was meant to be able to afford, I simply take a tuck here, a nip there, and make everything better.

But take care. Some photos, despite your best indentations, are simply not worth trying to save. In one attempt to improve my profile in an otherwise decent photograph, I ended up cutting off my nose to spite my face. Oh, and this reminds me: Never underestimate the benefits of a well-placed sticker.

I'm telling you, these photosensitive secrets will change the way you look at yourself for the rest of your emboldened and embellished life.

True Lives of Scrapbookers #2: The Final Cut

[Author's note: Some people find it necessary to create scrapbooks for every event, blessed or not, in their lives. Basket case in point: the woman who wrote this while coming to terms with her divorce.]

I am a seasoned scrapper with time and age spots on my hands, which is why my collection of scrapbooks is always completely up-to-date. I scrapbook for myself and I scrapbook for others; I have scrapbooked every stage of life from precradle (albums containing nothing but my friends' babies' ultrasound images) to grave gatherings (funeral ceremonies—the fact that they call them *memorial* services is a call to action for scrappers like me). Some might say I am overzealous in this way but I don't believe a scrapbooker can be too overzealous.

Recently, I went slightly mental when my marriage ended. It was as life-altering an experience as anything you can imagine, which, in my opinion, made it an event worthy of visual documentation. When I mentioned to my scrapbooker friend that I was going to create a divorce album documenting the ups and downs (well, the downs, anyway, since there were no ups) of my marriage ending, she winced and said it was demoralizing to have divorce photos in the first place, and in a scrapbook they had NO place.

Nonsense! I thought, or said, or wrote in red glittery ink across the cover of my Divorce Scrapbook. What could it possibly hurt to focus one final time on the most destructive event of my life here on earth? Who would it harm? Not me! In fact it would be nothing but a cathartic festival for me.

The funny thing is I was not the least bit bitter about my divorce. Sad? Sure. Hurt? Naturally. Surprised? Quite. But bitter? Nope, not that I recall. [Author: A restraining order says otherwise, but this is her side of the story and chances are she is going to read this, so never mind.] How utterly strange to have my heart broken and my home shattered in the same week. It was a week a weaker person would just as soon forget, but I felt strongly that it would be important to document the bad and the ugly events in my otherwise good life. So through it all I shot photos of the life-sucking event.

Once I got beyond my divorce and the healing began, out came my divorce photographs. There on the table in a pile of disorder were images showing the undoing of my well-being. Lookie here, the photos seemed to say, here is a spitting image of sorrow. And here, and here. This is what divorce looks like; and this. Suddenly I had a white-knuckle grip on my Fiskars scissors as I wrestled with the realization that bad things happen to good people. What to do with this new bout of rage? Work through it, that's what. Scrapbook the hell out of it.

Calmly, I organized the photographs. First there was the image of my husband—or my "ex-husband" as they like to say in divorce court—all innocent looking, without so much as a worry in the world. Very amusing, that photo. Amusing because later that day, there in our cozy kitchen, he will tell me he doesn't love me, he never loved me, he loves another woman, and he is leaving me to be with her. "Here! Take this with you!" I will say as I fling Mr. Garlic, a small but heavy glass figurine, across the kitchen at my husband, who will be too stunned to duck. This explains why, in the next photo, the photo where he is looking up at the second-floor window from which his personal belongings are being tossed, he has the swollen nose.

Then there was the "irrefutable proof" photo. Why I still had this shot—a shot to the heart—who knew? It is a picture of the red-handed man who was married to me with a coldhearted woman who is clearly not me; a woman who is unquestionably someone who has had her teeth whitened a few too many times. What's wrong with this picture? (Besides the obvious, I mean.) Its focus and composition are not what you would shoot for, but, according to the private investigator, the lighting was terrible and he had no choice but to use a high-powered zoom lens.

If forced to pick, I'd say my favorite divorce photo was the one taken in my lawyer's office. It was our final time together as a couple and there I sat with my camera while my husband sat reading the final divorce papers, which increasingly upset him as he came to understand that my lawyer was more savvy than his lawyer. Just as he started ranting, I snapped his picture and caught on film the rarely photographed desperate look of a man whose financial stability is slip-sliding away.

Next there were the photos of his hairy back and a few close-ups of his left upper arm, eczema and all. Not that they had a thing to do with the divorce, no, these pictures simply served as reminders of what I would not much miss about him.

Then, a most unexpected thing happened. As I looked over the accumulation of photos documenting the demise of my marriage, my anger dissolved into sadness. Who was I to judge another person's heart or behavior? Let it go, I thought, as I began to crop away at the photographs. A snip here, a snip there, until the divorce images were in shreds—scraps, if you will—to be forgotten and all forgiven. [Author: She used the photo shreds to line the bottom of her bird's cage; nevertheless, her change of heart was genuine.]

Then, project complete, I playfully threw the scissors out the window, which fortunately was open. The cropping experience left me exhausted but at peace. I believe there's a sweet irony in all of this, if you want to hear it. [Editor: We don't! XO!]

CHAPTER 38

True Lives of Scrapbookers #3: Using the Ol' Noodle

[Author's note: Here's a unique idea from a creative scrapbooking sister who needs to get out more.]

Mama mia, I like pasta. Some I like hot, some I like cold. Some I like glued on a scrapbook page.

The pasta-on-paper idea I got from my child's preschool. Years ago, she came home with a Christmas tree ornament that was precious, sure, since her little hands had made it; and clever, very, inasmuch as her preschool had made it for next to nothing despite their monthly $30 fee for arts and crafts supplies, which in this instance amounted to macaroni stuck on a flat, doodled piece of dandy cardboard. Not since November's toothpick turkey had I seen such a shameless display of minimalism in art. (On the other hand, those Montessori teachers taught my daughter to tie her shoes and play well with others, both invaluable skills that continue to benefit her on a daily basis.)

Every Christmas, year in and year out, that little macaroni ornament came out of the ornament box none the worse for wear. Which was a good thing, as I considered its pasta embellishments an emergency food source.

So, last year I developed an appetite for scrapbooking. I ended up in an arts and crafts store tossing item after item into my shopping cart. The last item on my list was "decorative embellishment," so I asked the sales assistant for suggestions. She rubbed at the silver embellishment adorning her left nostril, drew a breath, and started in, "We've got jimjams, screaming meemies, beezie-weezies, giddy goodies, upsy-daisies, wiggle-waggles, teeny-weenies, itsy-bitsies, yellow polka dots . . ." and here's where I tried to interrupt, but she went on and ended with ". . . plus sugar pie poodle pants."

"Did you say poodle?" I asked. When I heard the word poodle, I thought noodle! I thought, "How about noodle embellishments?"

Several days and many pasta shapes later I was exhausted yet exhilarated from all the noodling. It was clear I was onto something—something that had to be the best embellishment idea to come along since sliced brads. Yet when I showed a scrapbooking friend my completed pasta pages she said, "Ohmygosh! You can't just go gluing macaroni onto otherwise perfectly good pages!"

"Can and will," I said.

And I have. Naturally, all of my scrapbooks are linguine-free since I feel the same way about linguine as I feel about lignin—won't have it near my scrapbooks. Linguine is too thick, too unwieldy, too life-threatening if you eat it covered in clam sauce and end up with a not-so-mild bout of food poisoning. (Which reminds me, since we are touching on the subject of pasta consumption: Italians recommend small portions and are, frankly, appalled by the heaping helpings of noodles we Americans pile on our plates. All I have to say to them regarding this is: "*Tu say tae-mato, yo say toe-mato*! E *amora*! A*mora*! The more-a the better!")

As far as I know, pasta has not been extensively researched by any sort of archival expert. So by all means, before you use any type of food, including noodles, in your scrapbooks, do some research. Despite my enthusiasm, my opinions do not take the place of thoughtful discussions with a scrapbooking professional. Meanwhile, keep in mind that if it all goes terribly wrong you have only yourself and possibly my daughter's preschool to blame.

For now, I hope you will find creative ways to freely enjoy any or all of these many marvelous suggestions for using macaroni as embellishments:

> Angel hair: Delicate pasta for hand lettering and swirl designs.
>
> Annellini: Pasta rings for circular motifs.
>
> Conch shells: Surf's up! Perfect for creating a beach theme.
>
> Orzo: Lovely wedding-page pasta for a ricelike adornment.

CHAPTER 39

True Lives of Scrapbookers #4: The Creative Type

[Author's note: I met this sweet-faced woman in a therapy group where I was doing research. Yes, that's right, research. She was new to scrapbooking and felt she had a story to tell. I disagreed, but who am I to disagree with someone so dangerously close to a nervous breakdown? So in her own words, here's her story.]

As I travel down life's highway I'm always on the lookout for some new creative adventure. Why? I was born to be wildy creative, that's why and that's me.

Surprisingly, I wasn't always the creative type. As a child—a child prodigy if you must know—I was the better-than-you type, believing as I did that my distant relatives were aristocrats. Then came a sobering, grim moment when I learned it was all a big misunderstanding and in actuality my European relatives were not aristocratic but artistic. It was not an easy thing to say "So long, farewell, *auf Wiedersehen*" to all that. I mean, how would *you* like it? One minute you're practically royalty and the next thing you know you are nothing but artistic. Which is something, don't get me wrong. I am thrilled to be better than everybody else when it comes to art.

Since that day, art has been my life, imitated my life, and vice versa, except on Sundays. This is why, last year, I jumped at the chance to take photos of my uncommon existence and turn them into art—which is how I came to be sitting in the Beginner's Scrapbook Class.

The instructor, while noticeably well-groomed and knowledgeable about scrapbooking, was obviously intimidated by my rarely seen artistic flair, which may explain but does not excuse her reason for ignoring my spectacular work of scrapbook art. In fact, I had no choice but to finally put my finished page right in her face and practically shout, "Well?"

And what was her response do you think? "*Brava!*" or "Exquisite!" or "Look, everyone! We have an artistic genius among us!"

No. All this poor excuse for an instructor said was, "Whoa! Interesting."

So I pointed at my innovative lettering and said, "What do you think of my innovative lettering?"

"Uh, not bad!" she said, patting my shoulder. "There's no cost if you'd like to repeat the class."

"What! What, may I ask, is your problem?" I said while abruptly standing. "Can't you see I'm arthritic," I cried, clawed hands in the air. Then, scooping up my scrapbooking supplies, I rushed out, shouting, "Excuse me, I mean artistic—and I shan't return!"

To help you better understand why I was shouting, some say shrieking, indignantly, you must first consider that I am an *artiste*. Artisans as a rule are temperamental. Half are emotional. Half are arrogant. The rest of us cannot suffer fools. You do the math. This is not to say you are better mathematically. All I am saying is, and bear in mind I wouldn't be saying anything at all about any of this were it not part of my anger management therapy, that none of us is better than any of us. Except for the special few of us who apparently were born to be creative, wildly so.

Like me, for example. When I see the work of other artists, I can't help but notice the ways my creation puts theirs to shame. How does this make me feel? Humble and grateful, that's how. Grateful for my artistic genes and humble because I am, after all, no longer an aristocrat—even though, in truth, I still feel superior.

And in conclusion, I just want to apologize to the scrapbooking teacher, whose name I don't know, for my outburst. I carry no small disgrace for the way I behaved. My brutal honesty was partly to blame, yet kindly keep in mind, as I mentioned before and I shall, no doubt, mention again: We artistic types are too emotional, too passionate to be judged by the standards of the rest of you. It's something you will never understand, so there.

CHAPTER 40

True Lives of Scrapbookers #5: Pet Project

[Author: This next essay is from an animal lover who wrote it while undergoing a series of rabies shots.]

Labor of love or pet project—pick a cliché. It was a dog scrapbook. Before you roll over and play dead or wonder aloud why anybody would devote her first scrapbook to a family pet, please, let me point out the obvious: You don't have a dog, dear. If you did you would know dogs can outrun, outjump, and out-fox any child. Dogs are also more loyal, more obedient, and better foot warmers than any husband.

As for yours truly, I am your classic Dog Ma; a mutt-er figure, so to speak. Speak! That brings up another good point: What child barks on command? My husband, aka Pup Daddy, has photographed the major events thus far in our dog's life, so we had litter-ally hundreds of photos in need of a good album. At the time my best friend, that is to say my *human* best friend, called to invite me to go with her to an arts and crafts class. She said I would be able to learn how to create a dog scrapbook while she was learning how to make a scrapbook for—*get this!*—her cat.

So I ended up taking my photos to a scrapbooking class. First, I had to be paper trained. Once I learned about color coordination and acid-free cardstock, I was cautioned to avoid non-photo-friendly paper at all costs, no matter how cute the pattern. The cheerful instructor went on to bark out a few more lessons before saying, "Now you're ready to create your first page!"

"Just like that? But how? You have yet to teach us about the creative process!" I pointed out.

The instructor just smiled and told me to simply unleash my artistic imagination. The fact that I lack artistic imagination was the challenge behind my decision to surround the photos on my scrapbook page with the dog hair that was, that day, covering my sweater and pants. Once I had every hair in place, or at least on the page, I added some Tic Tacs, a pad of wax, and I gave that dog a bone!

Going with a dog theme without going too far was a creative challenge! Yet I felt it ended up somehow working and was well worth the effort. As a final touch I dog-eared the corners of the page after adding titles such as: "Puppy Dog Tales"; "Let Sleeping Dogs Lie"; "Bitch! Bitch! Bitch!"; "Puppy Love"; and "Hot Dogs!" I was just about to reward myself with a well-earned treat when I noticed the class instructor standing behind me scratching behind her right ear. I was ready to take a bow.

"Wow!" she shouted, picking up my scrapbook page from the table and looking at it as if she had just lifted her foot and found dog poop on the bottom of her shoe. Slowly, without taking her eyes from the page, she reached over and took away my scissors. "I must say your methods of design are unusual," she said kindly. "Very unusual! Well, how about you start over from scratch and this time we'll keep you on a shorter leash!"

Despite the rough, rough layouts, the finished scrapbook was fetching. Sure, the excessive play on canine-related words and page titles on every page was obnoxious to non–animal lovers, but overall the entire project made me rather happy. So happy, in fact, that I'm now considering creating scrapbooks for my children. That is just how rabid I am about scrapbooking.

One thing all of these "real life" scrapbookers made clear is that their scrapbooks express their personalities. Few things are more personal and unique than your cherished moments preserved on scrapbook pages created by you.

The thrill of scrapbooking is that you know your albums, your memories, your treasures are yours and yours alone. You can share them, but only you get to keep them.

CHAPTER 41

The Essence of Scrapbooking

Let me tell you, it felt good to write this book about scrapbooking. It felt really good—that is, until I realized something was missing. Something I was unable to put my finger on but felt in my heart was the essence of scrapbooking. Why now, when I was so close to calling it quits, did it suddenly dawn on me that there was something more essential to be said even though all I really wanted to do was go fly a kite, take a hike, or jump in a lake? Really, I could have just kicked myself. But why kick myself when there are others standing by waiting to kick in, come to the rescue, as it were, help me sum up, in anywhere from seven hundred to one thousand words, the quintessential meaning of scrapbooking? Any one of my friends or family members, I felt sure, would help me zero in on the "essence" I had somehow overlooked. How utterly disturbing, then, when I phoned my scrapbook-loving friends and family and was told more or less,

"Sorry, I already gave at the office." Not even my sisters were eager to help me one last time.

One of them simply said, "No." Another one said, "Hell, no." [Editor: Actually, what I said was, "No, no, and hell, no!"]

So, I called my older sister, the one who always had the most scraps of wisdom anyway, the one who has a genius for scrapbooking and a genuine desire to share her gift. She is such a good person and scrapbooker that when she walks into a room people will say, "Well, if it isn't one of the most gifted scrapbookers on earth!" So when I called her I said, "Hello! Is that you? One of the world's most gifted scrapbookers?" I was surprised to discover that although blood may be thicker than water, she is nobody's fool. She is not someone on whom you can use flattering words more than once to trick her into writing an essay about scrapbooking, even if you mention it is the most important essay of the book, the one that covers the heart and soul, the essence, if you will, of scrapbooking. "I will not help you any more with your book, stop calling me in the middle of the night."

Well, essays regarding essence don't just write themselves, so I called the one person who I knew would never dare refuse my pleas for help. "Mother?" I said. "What is the essence of scrapbooking?"

I had asked her similar questions before, but this time I was willing to listen to her answer; this time I was sitting at my computer, hands poised over the keyboard. "What is at the heart of your scrapbooking obsession? In short," I asked her point-blank, "Why do you scrap?"

"Well, as I have told you before, scrapbooking thoroughly entertains me; it makes me laugh out loud. It's inspiring. It makes me feel good about my life and the people in my life; it probably improves my sex life, though I don't want you to repeat that."

Oops.

"When I scrapbook, time stands still," she waxed on. "It's like I sit down to create a page and I lose all sense of time. It's wonderful, very therapeutic. Scrapbooking itself is a very effective form of psychotherapy. Furthermore, it grounds me."

"Grounds you?" I asked for clarification. "Grounds you as in you say to yourself, 'I'm grounded! *Got that*? Grounded! I told me not to spend so much money and time on scrapbooking, and then I went right ahead and did anyway. So now I forbid me from leaving this house for a week!' "

Stifling a smile, I waited for my mother to laugh. But she showed restraint, as she always does when I say something hilarious, and instead continued counting the ways she loved scrapbooking: "Scrapbooking also helps me find answers to the big questions in life: Where did I come from? Where am I going? What does it all mean?"

"Well, call Grandma. She'll tell you where you're going. And while you've got her on the phone ask her for me where ants go at night."

That's been the big question on my mind lately: Where do these five (sometimes there have been as many as seven) reddish-brown ants in my medicine cabinet come from, and where do they go at night? Every morning it is like some strange phenomenon to find ants just wandering around the base of the bottle of mouthwash I keep there for emergencies. Then, at night, when I reach for the toothpaste, the ants are always gone. Vanished. You cannot bring yourself to wipe out these peace-dwelling ants because you know they likely built a great colony, or at least a farm, in their youth. When I observe these ants I think life is a miracle; it's a miracle, really, that something as small as an ant can give birth. Still, I want to know how they keep finding their way into my house. Soon I will stop wondering and send them on a new adventure.

So back to scrapbooking. We all know what our mothers mean when they say scrapbooking helps them value what's important in life. When I stare at some of the pictures of my children, my heart swells and I can't help but wonder, what sort of person will he grow up to be? Where is he going? To Tampa, Florida, maybe? Or Mesa, Arizona? And if so, will he remember to pack clean underwear? I always expect good things from others, always hope for the best. Excuse me for candidly admitting it, but my gift is my ability to see the potential for good in everybody; yes, that's where my genius lies. [Editor: She lies about her genius.] Maybe she's right, although she has this tendency to be wrong often.

There is, now that I think about it, something profound I know that I did not realize I knew a few minutes ago; something that I suddenly realize has changed my life and made me a better person, a happier, kinder, more loving person, a person who now may or may not refuse to talk or associate with others who were unwilling to give a mile when I asked for an inch. What I have learned about scrapbooking, I have known since I began writing this book. The essence of scrapbooking is this: It can save lives. Scrapbookers are, in essence, lifesavers. They save life's memories from fading away by creating original legacies of love. That's it. That's all we need to know.